The Quiz QUIZ
By Brian Highley

First published Kindle 2019
First published paperback 2019

ISBN: 9781712144893

Dedicated to Jude, Milo, Adam, Harrison and Lilah

Quiz Setting

If you are preparing a quiz for teams you should take into consideration that several brains hold many times more information than one. The collective number of categories in which a group, let's say four people, have knowledge means that your quiz questions need to step up several notches in difficulty. If, on the other hand, your quiz is for individuals you should select easier questions or maybe even invent a couple of wrong answers for each question so they have a much easier multiple-choice situation. (My Multiple-Choice Quiz Book is due out soon.)

This book contains more popular culture questions (movies, TV, pop music) than other categories as experience and feedback show these to be the most popular with quizzers. Most categories have questions spread across the age groups so some will suit all ages. You know your own audience and should select questions accordingly. Not much point majoring on Rag'n'bone Man and Stormzy if you are quizzing in a senior citizens' care home, although I do know one O.A.P. whose favourite video is 'Roar' by Katy Perry but I'm not sure this is down to the music!

The questions here are designed for you to mix and match your own categories. For example a Music category might take individual questions from the various Pop categories in the book with a few Classical and Movie Musicals thrown in for variety. There are multiple Science and Nature categories

from which to select questions to make your own invidualised selection. Your Geography category could pick from the various country pages, etc.

Make sure the teams have paper and pens to record their answers. Teams should nominate a captain to make decisions in case of disputes. Don't make your quiz too long. A pub quiz of six categories with ten questions in each should last around an hour and forty-five minutes allowing time for a fifteen minute loo and beer break.

Read out each question twice. At the end of every round ask if anyone would like a question repeating and then swap papers for marking. I'm not suggesting people will cheat but if you wait until half time or the very end of the session before marking you might notice some players popping out for a quick Google. I recommend politely asking people to turn off their mobile phones. Many people know of my link with Trivial Pursuit and you would be amazed by the number of evening texts and calls I receive asking for advice on obscure facts and I'm sure these are all from friends taking part in pub quizzes.

Always have a tie-breaker ready. A selection can be found at the end of this book. A good tie-breaker is a difficult question with a numerical answer making the winner the person or team whose guess is closest to being correct.

And don't take quizzing too seriously, after all, the name of the game is TRIVIA !!

. . . .

1. What is your bad habit if you are described as an onychophagist?

2. Which parts of the human body are surrounded by protective skin called eponychium and paranychium?

3. Which syndrome, taking its name from a European city, sees hostages bonding with their captors?

4. Where will you find epicanthic folds?

5. Which term for an abnormal sac of fluid comes from a Greek word meaning bladder?

6. What was known as French Pox in Tudor times?

7. What percentage of the average human bodyweight is bone?

8. What is borborygmi the technical word for?

9. What is the common name for the toe deformity hallux valgus?

10. What did our early ancestors produce by mixing animal fat with wood ash?

11. Which is the fastest growing human tissue?

12. How many times bigger than the average fist is the average heart?

13. What percentage of your DNA do you share with a banana?

14. Where did a 2010 survey reveal that 27% of British couples first met?

15. What do people tend to rush to if they suffer a gastrocolic reflex?

16. What does an autotonsorialist do that most women are willing to pay for?

17. Where are the fastest acting muscles in the human body?

18. What is the common term for emesis?

19. What are cut in the process known as exungulation?

20. What is hyperhidrosis the excessive production of?

1. Which Canadian-born cosmetic queen's real name was Florence Nightingale Graham?

2. To what did the Children's Supermarket change its name?

3. What became known as deeples in the 1950s?

4. Who is best known for designing a cowboy hat and had the middle name Batterson?

5. What should the average Big Mac have 178 of?

6. How many flowers decorate each side of a standard Oreo cookie?

7. Which drink was invented in 1873 by Philadelphia druggist Charles Hires?

8. What is fashion designer Givenchy's first name?

9. What is traditionally sipped from a copita glass?

10. What name is given to the loop closest to the buckle of a belt?

11. Which clothing company is hyped: 'Lets you laugh at the weather'?

12. What colourful name did the Minnesota Valley Canning Company adopt?

13. What does a muselet hold in place?

14. Which food chain was launched in 1937 by Vernon Carver Rudolph?

15. 'Save the Planet' is the motto of which international restaurant chain?

16. Who launched slippers in 2015 that cost £1,200 per pair and were described as looking like guinea pigs?

17. Which Emperor is connected with Empire Style?

18. Which iconic British clothing items did Samantha Cameron take as gifts for the Obama children on a 2010 U.S. visit?

19. Who did L.A. Gear attempt to sue for reportedly refusing to wear their trainers while making a commercial for them?

20. Why is Yarg cheese so called?

1. What was the sleepy five-letter Allied code name for Pearl Harbor in World War II?

2. The name of which famed thoroughfare did Alcatraz inmates give to the main cell-block corridor?

3. Which future King was dubbed Edward the Caresser?

4. What punishment was introduced to the U.K. by the 1972 Criminal Justice Act?

5. Which is the world's oldest, ongoing annual civic parade?

6. What did Davy Crocket know as Betsy?

7. To what does the Seventh Amendment give Americans the right?

8. What's the better known name of the British queen whose first name was actually Alexandrina?

9. Which principality was once called Fort Hercules?

10. By how many seats did the Tories fall short of an overall majority in the 2017 June election?

11. What did Albino Luciani become for 33 days in 1978?

12. Who was England's 'Merry Monarch'?

13. Which U.S. President did Sara Jane Moore attempt to assassinate?

14. Which U.S. President was dubbed the Comeback Kid?

15. What practical use was found for the White House lawn during World War I?

16. What was the relationship between President W.H. Taft and Pauline Wayne?

17. The name of which location is spelt incorrectly on the Liberty Bell?

18. Whose abduction by Paris started the Trojan War?

19. By what name is frontierswoman Martha Jane Canary better known?

20. Who was the Babington Plot intending to assassinate?

. . . .

1. Which album that achieved astronomical sales was almost titled 'Eclipse'?

2. What is Maxwell's inventive surname in the Beatles' song 'Maxwell's Silver Hammer'?

3. What's the better-known name of the rock 'n' roll pioneers who were once called The Downhomers and then became The Saddlemen?

4. Which folk-rock singer-songwriter has the middle name Chandos?

5. Who is the first movie star name-checked in the Kinks' song 'Celluloid Heroes'?

6. In what song does Bob Dylan ask nine rhetorical questions?

7. How many songs are there on Elvis Presley's 1974 album 'Having Fun with Elvis on Stage'?

8. In which song does Bill Withers repeat the phrase 'I know' 26 consecutive times?

9. What was Stevie Wonder's Oscar-winning song from 'The Woman in Red'?

10. Which quartet consisted of Johnny Cash, Waylon Jennings, Kris Kristofferson and Willie Nelson?

11. Whose spoof discography includes albums titled 'Intravenus de Milo' and 'Smell the Glove'?

12. In the lyric of 'Jailhouse Rock' who plays tenor sax?

13. Which early rock 'n' roller was dubbed 'The Killer'?

14. Who called herself Bonnie Jo Mason early in her career?

15. To what Texas city was the plane flying in the original title of what became Gladys Knight's 'Midnight Train to Georgia'?

16. What's the first car name-checked in the lyric of Blondie's song 'Rapture'?

17. The hit song 'Best That You Can Do' comes from which movie?

18. Which instrument did Stuart Sutcliffe play with the Beatles?

19. Which city was the birthplace of Rod Stewart and Phil Collins?

20. Which member of Dr Zoom and the Cosmic Boom progressed to a stellar solo career?

• •

1. Which nation knocked England out of the 2018 World Cup?

2. What was once known as a battledore?

3. What was Muhammad Ali's final fight theatrically dubbed?

4. Which country's athletes sport the letters TTO on their vests?

5. What prize is handed to the winner of the British Golf Open?

6. For how many seconds must a rodeo rider stay onboard in the bareback riding event?

7. Which sport's rules require competitors to throw an object weighing no more than two pounds ten ounces?

8. How many balls does each team throw per frame in the game of Bocce?

9. Which word does the referee shout between 'crouch' and 'set' when organising a Rugby Union scrum?

10. Which Wimbledon winner was dubbed the Ice Maiden?

11. Which sport does Fred Astaire play while dancing in the movie 'Carefree'?

12. Which sport was once known as minonette?

13. Which sport is reported on the radio during Meat Loaf's hit song 'Paradise by the Dashboard Light'?

14. Who is by far the best-known member of the Pin Pals bowling team?

15. What's the name for a logrolling tournament?

16. What do golfers measure with a Stimp Meter?

17. What is the tennis term for a straight-set shutdown match of 6-0, 6-0, 6-0?

18. Which sport star named her pet Yorkshire Terrier Pete, after Pete Sampras?

19. Who titled his autobiography, 'The Greatest Game of All'?

20. Which game is played by the Memphis Grizzlies?

. . . .

1. Which hugely popular stage and movie musical features an ice cream parlour hangout called the Frosty Palace?

2. Which timely piece of music by Ponchielli is heard in Disney's 'Fantasia'?

3. 'Hefty Hideaway, the House of Fashion for the Ample Woman' is a feature of which musical?

4. Which English shipping port gives its name to the horse on which Eliza Doolittle places a bet in 'My Fair Lady'?

5. In which musical movie does Bing Crosby's character pen a song called 'Choo Choo Mama'?

6. What was the follow-up movie to 'Saturday Night Fever'?

7. Which of Richard Wagner's operas requires the sound of 18 anvils?

8. Which musical's characters include Julie Jordan, a worker at Bascombe Cotton Mills?

9. Eighteen dancers vying for eight jobs provides the plot for which popular musical?

10. Which hip musical's London run ended abruptly in 1973 when the theatre roof collapsed?

11. Which seasonal song that provided a hit for Tom Jones is from the musical 'Neptune's Daughter'?

12. Which famed bandleader's first name was Alton?

13. Which musical included the Academy Award-winning song 'The Continental'?

14. How many cornets join the Big Parade in the 'Seventy Six Trombones' song from 'The Music Man'?

15. Which composer is the subject of the movie 'Immortal Beloved'?

16. What birthday is Annie about to celebrate when she sings the song 'Tomorrow'?

17. Which movie introduced the Academy Award-winning song 'It's Hard Out Here for a Pimp'?

18. What is the nickname of Haydn's seventh symphony?

19. Who was pictured on the back of the UK £20 note withdrawn in 2012?

20. Which musical's songs include 'Naughty' and 'Revolting Children'?

. . . .

1. In which sport did Jade Jones win gold for Britain at the 2016 Olympics?
2. How many Olympics have been cancelled due to war?
3. What is the fruity nickname of Olympic gold medal snowboarder Shaun White?
4. Which is the longest race in the women's Olympic heptathlon?
5. What was the name of the unidentifiable creature that was the 1996 Atlanta Olympics mascot?
6. Which Olympic sport's playing surface measures nine feet by five feet?
7. What was Rosemary Ackerman's gold medal-winning sport?
8. How many seconds are on the Olympic basketball shot clock?
9. What did Emperor Hirohito give to swimmer Dawn Frazer after she was banned for stealing one from his palace?
10. What was the accepted energy snack of the 1992 Olympics?
11. How many times have the summer Olympics been held in the USA?
12. What crisp nickname was given to the 2012 London Olympics velodrome?
13. What is the surname of British rowers Jonny and Greg who won Olympic gold medals in 1992?
14. What other prize is British silver-medalist Philip Noel-Baker the only Olympian to have won?
15. What was French athlete Constantin Henriquez de Zubiera's Olympic first in 1900?
16. What was unique about the measurements at the 1904 St Louis Olympics?
17. Which country has won the lowest number of Olympic medals per capita?
18. Under how many different flags has shooter Jasna Sekarics competed in the Olympics?
19. In which sport did England's Charlotte Cooper become the Olympics' first woman champion?
20. What was the first team sport to feature in the Olympics?

1. Which novel sees the tiny Duchy of Grand Fenwick declare war on the USA?

2. Which traveller visits a land of magicians and sorcerers called Glubdubrib?

3. Which Dickens character lodges at the George and Vulture Inn when he visits London?

4. What colour horse is ridden by Pestilence, one of the Four Horsemen of the Apocalypse?

5. What are the weather conditions when the Invisible Man arrives at Bramblehurst Station?

6. What is the surname of Kingsley Amis' character 'Lucky Jim'?

7. A village called Hayslope is central to the plot in which novel by George Eliot?

8. 'Headlong' by Ellyn Williams is the inspiration for which movie?

9. Which 1969 Oscar-winner is based on a novel by James Leo Herlihy?

10. Albus Dumbledore's pet, named Fawkes in the 'Harry Potter' books, is what kind of creature?

11. Whose comic book enemies include the Draconians?

12. What is the timely surname of the main family in 'The Borrowers'?

13. Which colourful author called himself James Aston during his early writing career?

14. 'Car-Boy-Girl' by Gordon Buford gave birth to which fast-moving movie franchise?

15. Which U.S. state is the setting for Walter Van Tilburg Clark's novel 'The Ox-Bow Incident'?

16. Which steamy novel features Compton's Café?

17. Who's the main character in books featuring the Cleansweep 7 Broomstick?

18. What's the name of the cat who returns from the dead in 'Pet Sematary'?

19. Which five-letter word found in many crime thrillers translates from the Latin for 'in another place'?

20. 'Autobiography of a Horse' is the subtitle of which novel?

1. Which American artist sculpted the Pink Panther embracing a large-breasted blonde lady?

2. What is the English name for the colour Vincent van Gogh knew as 'geel'?

3. What name have Americans given to the black and white logo designed in 1958 for the Campaign for Nuclear Disarmament?

4. For which branch of the arts is France's annual Moliere Award presented?

5. Which painter/photographer titled his autobiography 'Self Portrait'?

6. Which famed artist worked for a time as a teacher at the Reverend William P. Stokes School in the English seaside resort of Ramsgate?

7. Which century saw the death of John Constable?

8. The Bargello Gallery is in which Italian city?

9. Which British Art Nouveau master famously illustrated 'Morte d'Arthur'?

10. Which letter did Pieter Breughel drop from his name?

11. The word 'limner' describes what type of artist?

12. Of what are calotypes early examples?

13. In which branch of the arts was code inventor Samuel Morse a respected exponent?

14. What is melted between wires on a copper base to produce cloisonné?

15. Which nationality was the great 18th century painter John Singleton Copley?

16. For which style of drawings were George and Isaac Cruikshank best known?

17. Who described his own works as, 'hand-painted dream photographs'?

18. What was the family relationship between Thomas Gainsborough and Gainsborough Dupont?

19. Which sport did American artist George Bellows most famously paint?

20. Which Post-Impressionist's death was blamed on the amputation of a gangrenous leg following complications caused by syphilis?

. . . .

1. What is the name of Alex's pet dog in 'Flashdance'?

2. In which movie does Keenan Wynn fill the role of Colonel Bat Guano?

3. Which movie sees Johnny propose to Loretta in the Grand Ticino restaurant?

4. What starry pseudonym does Marty McFly adopt in 'Back to the Future III'?

5. Which brand of doll is Chucky in 'Child's Play'?

6. What is the name of Dan Ackroyd's 'Ghostbusters' character?

7. Which of the Bond movies sees Mr Big distributing drugs at the Fillet of Soul restaurant?

8. Which movie's cantina band is called Figrin D'an and the Modal Nodes'?

9. In 'Toy Story 2' what is the name of the toy store?

10. Alphabetically, who start with Tasso Bravos and end with Joseph Wladislaw?

11. What two-letter command do the humans give to the apes in 'Conquest of the Planet of the Apes'?

12. Which reggae icon is the voice of Ernie, the jellyfish, in 'Shark's Tail'?

13. What was hyped: 'A family comedy without the family'?

14. What is the name of the gang's pet restaurant in 'American Pie'?

15. Herbie and the Heartbeats feature in which retro-rock musical movie?

16. What is Ted and Alice's surname in 'Bob and Carol, Ted and Alice'?

17. What's the name of the robot with Joan Rivers' voice in 'Spaceballs'?

18. Who says his favourite ice cream is Dragonfly Ripple?

19. For which of his novels does Charles Dickens inexplicably receive a credit at the end of 'Airplane'?

20. In 'Batman', which character asks: 'Did you ever dance with the devil in the pale moonlight'?

. . . .

1. Which 'Sesame Street' hero has a girlfriend named Grungetta?

2. What's the name of the pink, opera singing bird on 'The Muppet Show'?

3. What is Seinfeld's favourite breakfast cereal?

4. Who says 'I hate meeces to pieces'?

5. What is Lily Munster's maiden name?

6. Whose all-purpose reply is 'Heavens to Murgatroyd'?

7. In which sci-fi series is 'felgecarb' an expletive?

8. Who refer to their swimming pool as 'the cement pond'?

9. Which musical family travelled in a vehicle with a bumper sticker warning; 'Careful - Nervous Mother Driving'?

10. Which sitcom's instrumental theme tune is titled 'Angela'?

11. What is MacGyver's first name?

12. In which county will you find Bedrock, home town of the Flintstones?

13. Which fashion magazine's offices provide the setting for the sitcom 'Just Shoot Me'?

14. What is the pharaonic name of Morticia's pet African Strangler plant in 'The Addams Family'?

15. Which TV show features a game called bouillabaseball, based on baseball but played with fish parts?

16. Which animated title character attends Bluffington School?

17. What is Argo in 'Xena; Warrior Princess'?

18. In 'Wiseguy' what's the name of the record company commandeered by Vinnie Terranova?

19. Angel Grove, California is the setting for which sci-fi TV series?

20. Badge number 235 belongs to which TV sleuth?

1. What is the common name for graphospasm, or scrivener's palsy?

2. Diastema is an unusually large gap between what?

3. Epistaxis is the common name for which messy problem?

4. How would most people refer to diplopia?

5. Cephalgia is a doctor's term for what?

6. Circadian dysrhythmia is called what by most high flyers?

7. Which sense does an anosmia sufferer lack?

8. What is the common name for rhinorrhea?

9. Why do sufferers from doraphobia tend not to have pet cats?

10. Taurophobia is a fear of what?

11. What is contained in the pericardium sac?

12. What's the common name for the zygomatic bone?

13. In 1998, where did scientists claim you should shine a torch to prevent jet lag?

14. What facial features do the auricularis muscles move?

15. What were bathing caps invented to prevent?

16. Which nerve carries signals from the brain to the retina?

17. Which of the five senses does a human develop first?

18. What is commonly abbreviated to CHF?

19. Which organ is inflamed if you are suffering from nephritis?

20. Which single product is the world's main source of salmonella poisoning?

1. Which animal is responsible for the most human deaths in Australia?

2. How many toes does a cuckoo have on each foot?

3. Which animal record is held by the Alpine Black Salamander?

4. Which animal is feared by a cynophobic?

5. What is a turtle's plastron?

6. Of what does a walrus have 18, a beaver 20 and a tiger 30?

7. What is a Thompson Seedless?

8. Which animal was the symbol of liberty in ancient Rome?

9. How fast does a cat's heart beat when compared with that of a human?

10. Which painful medical condition are Dalmatian's the only breed of dog to contract?

11. Which insect was the subject of the first book ever to be written in Welsh?

12. Which fruit do bats most commonly pollinate?

13. Which animal is the symbol of the British Wildlife Trust?

14. Which bird is the national symbol of China?

15. A group of apes is known by what collective noun?

16. Chinese, Black Caiman and American are all varieties of what?

17. Which is the only animal with oval blood cells?

18. Which country added the Yeti to its protected species list in 1958?

19. For how many consecutive days does the average domestic cat remain on heat?

20. What is a Slippery Dick?

1. What did grocer Sylvan Goldman invent in 1924 for the convenience of his customers?

2. What does the WD stand for in the name of the product WD-40?

3. How many columns of beads make up a standard Chinese abacus?

4. The Acme Thunderer is the world's best-selling example of what?

5. Which motor manufacturer's name is Japanese for '50 Bells'?

6. What was 1955's Flashmatic the first wireless example of?

7. What is the longest unit of distance in astronomy?

8. For which element is hydragyrum the Latin name?

9. What is the internet suffix for the United Arab Emirates?

10. What does the 'R' stand for in MRI Scan?

11. Which element takes its chemical symbol, NA, from its former name?

12. How many pins connect a SCART plug?

13. Which type of paint is technically known as calcimine?

14. In which type of medication is simethicone a common ingredient?

15. What does the 'H' stand for in VHS?

16. What is the alternative name from tungsten from which it gets its chemical symbol W?

17. Who is the patron saint of astronomers?

18. For what did Emil Behring discover a serum that won him a Nobel Prize for medicine?

19. How many Concordes were built?

20. What comes in varieties including ribbon, staccato and bead?

1. Which famous American military man's first name is simply the letter H?
2. Which major movie actor's surname is Fowler?
3. Who is dubbed the Divine Miss M?
4. What title did John Sentamu take in 2005?
5. Who is lead vocalist on the 1999 CD titled 'Abba Pater'?
6. Which of Elizabeth II's children is the Earl of Inverness?
7. Which first name is common to singer LeAnn Rimes and the title character in 'Lady Windermere's Fan'?
8. At what age was John Lennon murdered?
9. Which item, once commonly seen in public places, did generous multimillionaire Paul Getty install at his English mansion for the use of guests?
10. What did Muhammad Ali, Stanley Kubrick and Ronald Reagan all admit to a fear of?
11. Which animal does Angelina Jolie have tattooed on her back?
12. What did Bing Crosby, Robert De Niro, Mel Gibson and Margaret Thatcher all have at estimated odds of 67 to 1?
13. What did Marlene Dietrich insure for $1 million?
14. Which religion was followed by David Bowie, Oliver Stone and Tina Turner?
15. Which U.S. state was the birthplace of Stevie Nicks, Linda Ronstadt and Geronimo?
16. Which university was attended by Bill Clinton, Oscar Wilde and Stephen Hawking?
17. Jennifer Aniston, Yoko Ono and Oprah Winfrey share which star sign?
18. Which is the country of birth of Joanna Lumley, George Orwell and Julie Christie?
19. What go alphabetically from Adeodatus to Zosimus?
20. What age did Sandra Bullock, Calista Flockhart and Nicholas Cage all reach in 2014?

• •

1. Where are you most likely to see the slogan 'annuit coeptis'?

2. What is the name of the female cat who Garfield tries to impress?

3. Which organisation has the slogan: 'A man may be down but he's never out'?

4. What does a plangonologist collect?

5. What colour is a UPS delivery van?

6. According to U.K. criminal law, what is the minimum number of people required for a riot?

7. Cerebra, the dog who guarded the entrance to Hades, had how many heads?

8. How many days and nights did Jonah spend in the belly of the whale?

9. Which is the largest city on the Mediterranean?

10. What creatures were Louie and Frankie in Budweiser commercials?

11. During which month of the year does the U.S. observe Pearl Harbor Remembrance Day?

12. Which mythical creature is the symbol of Reader's Digest?

13. Which condiment ingredient was the first thing marketed by Heinz?

14. What did Aztecs consider to be the excrement of the gods?

15. How many years are celebrated by a sesquicentennial?

16. Of what was 'The Original' the first purpose-built example?

17. What punctuation point first appeared in J. Day's 16th century 'Catechism of Edward VI'?

18. From which wood are most hot tubs constructed?

19. What is Pandalon in Hindu mythology?

20. Which item of an artist's equipment is depicted by the Pictor constellation?

1. Which card game is 007 playing when he insists Goldfinger must deliberately lose $15,000 after catching him cheating?

2. What is the highest score in baccarat?

3. How many coloured circles are there on a standard Twister mat?

4. What is the points bonus for using seven Scrabble tiles in one go?

5. Which is the only Pac-Man ghost with a name that doesn't rhyme with 'Inky'?

6. Which game was hyped: 'A minute to learn, a lifetime to master'?

7. What is the U.S. equivalent of Mayfair, the U.K.'s most expensive Monopoly property?

8. Which popular video game is known in Japan as 'Bokujo Monogatari,' or 'The Farm Story'?

9. What does Lando Cairissian win in a card game called Sabaac in 'The Empire Strikes Back'?

10. Which pinball mechanism was originally known as 'Stool Pigeon'?

11. Which rock star paid $15,000 in a charity auction to play chess against Gary Kasparov?

12. Which game did Nicolai Ceausescu ban from Romania because he deemed it too intellectual?

13. Which is the lowest ranking Bridge suit?

14. How much money do the rules require to be placed at the centre of a Monopoly board at the start of each game?

15. Which casino game features an insurance line?

16. How many cards are dealt to each player at the start of Gin Rummy?

17. Which was the first country after The U.S. and Canada to have its own Trivial Pursuit game?

18. What's your score if you roll cock-eyes at craps?

19. Which card game was devised by Harold Vanderbilt in 1925?

20. At what board game was Humphrey Bogart an expert?

1. Which is the largest and oldest still-inhabited castle in the world?

2. What time is it in Lisbon if it's noon in London on Christmas Day?

3. What was the former name of Mali?

4. At which position do the Himalayas appear on a list of the world's longest mountain ranges?

5. 'The Gateway to Europe' is the nickname of which city?

6. Which U.S. tourist magnet is dubbed 'The biggest little city in the world'?

7. Which tourist town has a name meaning 'Plain of dense reeds'?

8. The flag of Cyprus depicts what branches?

9. Which Californian city is served by John Wayne Airport?

10. Which African country attracted the most tourists in 2014, according to a U.N. report?

11. In which capital city will you find Tahir Square?

12. Which sea washes the beaches of Albania?

13. Which currency should tourists take to Andorra?

14. What colour are the bottom and top stripes on the flag of Argentina?

15. Which is world's largest riverless country?

16. On which gulf will you find Benin?

17. Which mountain range runs through little Liechtenstein?

18. Which city takes tourists to the Temple of Heaven?

19. In which country does the River Wand join the River Ping in a place called Tak?

20. Which Florida city is dubbed the Million Dollar Sandbar?

• •

1. Which member of the Kennedy family died in the same year as Martin Luther King Jr and Yuri Gagarin?

2. Which former U.S. President died in the same year as Judy Garland and Rolling Stone Brian Jones?

3. Which year saw the deaths of Charles de Gaulle, Jimi Hendrix and Janis Joplin?

4. Which year saw the deaths of J.R.R. Tolkien, Noel Coward and Bruce Lee?

5. Which year saw the deaths of T-Rex glam rocker Marc Bolan, Charlie Chaplin and Elvis Presley?

6. Which year saw the deaths of Pope Paul IV, Pope John Paul I and Keith Moon who was never the pope?

7. Which year saw the deaths of Josef Mengele, John Wayne and Sid Vicious?

8. Which major rock star died in the same year as Peter Sellers and Alfred Hitchcock?

9. Who was the most famous Jamaican to die in the same year as Natalie Wood and Bill Haley?

10. Which year saw the deaths of Rock Hudson, Orson Welles and Phil Silvers?

11. Which nasty Nazi committed suicide in the year Fred Astaire and Andy Warhol died?

12. Which year saw the deaths of Emperor Hirohito, Irving Berlin and Salvador Dali?

13. Which year saw the deaths of Miles Davis, Dr Seuss and Freddie Mercury?

14. Which year saw the deaths of Francis Bacon, Isaac Asimov and Benny Hill?

15. Which year saw the deaths of Arthur Ashe, Audrey Hepburn and Frank Zappa?

16. Which year saw the deaths of Burt Lancaster, Kurt Cobain and John Candy?

17. Whose death received by far the greatest outpouring of media coverage in the year Gianni Versace and Mother Teresa died?

18. Which year saw the deaths of Sonny Bono, Tammy Wynette and Frank Sinatra?

19. Which year saw the deaths of Perry Como, Jack Lemmon and George Harrison?

20. Which Bee Gee died in the same year as Barry White and Bob Hope?

• •

1. Which king was the losing leader at the Battle of Bannockburn?

2. Which U.S. President said: 'It is better to be alone than in bad company'?

3. What is the modern name for the Greek island known to ancient Romans as Candia?

4. In which decade did the world's population first pass the two billion mark?

5. In what decade did the world's population first pass the six billion mark?

6. Which country did Algeria become a part of in 1848?

7. In which decade was Andorra first recognised as a sovereign state?

8. What became the main crop of Barbados in the 17th century?

9. Which is Africa's oldest democracy?

10. Which was the first company to find oil in the North Sea?

11. What was the official language of England from 1099 to 1399?

12. In 2002, which country was loaned $30 billion over 15 months by the IMF?

13. Which country granted asylum to WikiLeaks founder Julian Assange?

14. The so-called 'soccer war' kicked off when which country was invaded by El Salvador?

15. Which was World War II's largest concentration camp?

16. What name was given to Germany's equivalent of Tokyo Rose?

17. How many U.S. Presidents served during the period Pierre Trudeau led Canada?

18. Which English admiral was dubbed The Dragon?

19. How did Stalin raise most of the money to fund the Russian Revolution?

20. Who placed the first phone call to the Moon?

. . . .

1. What are the people of North Korea required to choose from a government-approved selection of 28?

2. What floral name was given to the tiny shoes designed for the shrunken feet of Chinese ladies?

3. Which word completes mini-skirt pioneer Mary Quant's quip; 'A woman is as old as her ....'?

4. What name is given to the phenomenon whereby a 1967 size-eight dress is now size-zero?

5. Which fashion house launched the Kelly Bag?

6. Which city saw the birth of the Rolex company?

7. Which worldwide clothing chain began in 1969 as a single unit in San Francisco selling only Levi jeans and L.P. records?

8. Which clothing item was invented and patented by Mark Twain?

9. What were the colours of Barbie's first swimsuit?

10. What activates GPSs programmable shoes?

11. What did Queen Elizabeth I make it a legal requirement for all women to wear on a Sunday?

12. Which colour of heels did Louis XIV decree only members of the royal court could wear?

13. What were the Russian military not supplied with until 2007?

14. What decoration did the U.S. Navy ban in 1909?

15. Which very famous person's underwear was stalker Edward Jones arrested for stealing on four occasions?

16. What does a grabologist collect?

17. Which, company more famous for women's garb, made the spacesuits for Armstrong and Aldrin?

18. What was the world's first designer logo?

19. Which rapper is co-owner and co-creator of the Rocawear clothing line?

20. Which of the four main fashion weeks comes first?

1. How many holes decorate a standard Ritz cracker?

2. What does a Spanish bar tender pop into your Martini if you request an aceituna?

3. Which nation invented the Frankfurter?

4. On which volcano are the grapes grown to produce Lacrima Christi (Tears of Christ) wine?

5. Which animal's head is pictured on a Gordon's Gin label?

6. Which beer made Milwaukee famous?

7. From what is a bouquet garni made?

8. Which spice should be dusted on a Brandy Flip?

9. Which cocktail takes its name from a town near Santiago in Cuba?

10. What is mixed with lime and cranberry juices for a Scarlett O'Hara cocktail?

11. What name is given to a mixture of Tia Maria and milk?

12. Which bird was the filling for a traditional squab pie?

13. What do Irish people know as a Gravy Ring?

14. Which U.S. state produces Jim Beam bourbon.

15. Which dish takes its name from a Catalan word for 'pan'?

16. Which annually hyped drink did a famed critic describe as having, 'A bouquet not unlike a French motorway cafe toilet?

17. Which country originated the Wiener Schnitzel?

18. Which nuts should be found in a Waldorf Salad?

19. Which liquid brought fame and fortune to the French town of Vergeze?

20. Which is the world's most popular ewe's milk cheese?

. . . .

1. What were One Republic counting in the title of a 2014 chart hit?

2. What is the stage name of Robert James Ritchie who collaborated with Sheryl Crow on the song 'Picture'?

3. Who had their first international hit with 'I Bet You Look Good on the Dancefloor'?

4. Who was the eighth to be born of the singing Jackson family?

5. Which Coldplay hit begins; ' Look at the stars, look how they shine for you'?

6. Who was the featured artist on Lady Gaga's hit 'Do What U Want'?

7. What is the stage name of New Zealand singer/songwriter Ella Marie Yelich-O'Connor?

8. Which band had their first two hits with 'Laura' and 'Comfortably Numb'?

9. Which animal provided a 2013 hit for Bruno Mars?

10. Who is the first singer mentioned in Arthur Conley's tribute hit 'Sweet Should Music'?

11. Which country crooner's first name is Troyal?

12. Who is the first name-checked retro-celebrity in Madonna's 'Vogue'?

13. Which of the Spice girls boasted the most tattoos?

14. Which movie resurrected the old hit song 'Love Is All Around'?

15. Who issued a statement announcing to the world that 'Automatic For the People' would not divorce them from their teeny bop fans?

16. Which was the first album to sell one million copies in the U.K.?

17. Which was the first Elton John album to reach number-one in the U.K. and the U.S.?

18. Whose 'Love Songs' was the first album to sell ten million copies?

19. What is pictured behind the guitar on the sleeve of Dire Straits' 'Brothers in Arms'?

20. Who went on to greater things after making his recording debut playing harmonica on Harry Belafonte's 'Midnight Special' album?

1. Which plaything is an easy catch in cricket?

2. What does a judo referee mean when he says 'Hajime'?

3. Which activity links the surnames Fletcher and Butts?

4. What is indicated by a yachtsman's masthead fly?

5. With what word does the starter start a rowing race?

6. What title is given to the front, middle position of a volleyball team?

7. What is the handicap of a scratch golfer?

8. In which sport can you hike when you've close hauled?

9. What is the Scotch in Hopscotch?

10. What would a golfer keep in his shag bag?

11. Which sport originated the phrase, 'Throw your hat into the ring'?

12. What has the ball struck if a cricket batsman is served a beamer?

13. What is a bluffie to an archer?

14. What's the lowest par golf hole on which it is possible to shoot a double-eagle?

15. Which old English sport originated the term 'crestfallen'?

16. Which sportsman's equipment can include a Hairy Mary?

17. Which sport's rankings go from jonokuchi to yokozuna?

18. Which sport's slang terms include 'sizzle the pits' and 'facial disgracial'?

19. To whom should the ball be passed when a soccer referee blows the final whistle?

20. What is the alternative term for rappelling?

1. 'The Flesh Failures' is the subtitle of which song from 'Hair'?

2. 'Higgins' Universal Alphabet' is a book that appears in which musical?

3. Which musical's title character is Professor Harold Hill?

4. What is the name of the teen restaurant hangout in 'Footloose'?

5. According to Eliza Doolittle what; 'Hardly ever happen' in 'Hartford, Hereford and Hampshire'?

6. Which song from 'Gigi' gave director Vincent Minnelli the title for his autobiography?

7. Which is the musical if a spell found in Naboomu helps England win the Second World War?

8. Which musical features siblings with the surname Pontipee?

9. If Lerner and Lowe 'Call the Wind Maria,' what do they call the rain?

10. Which Brooklyn disco is the setting for the dance sequences in 'Saturday Night Fever'?

11. What colour dresses are worn by all the females on the 'Sound of Music' album sleeve with the exception of Julie Andrews?

12. Which musical, inspired by the Harlem Cotton Club, saw cameo appearances by Tony Braxton and k.d. lang?

13. 'Based on a book by Berry Gordy and including more than fifty songs', is a description of which musical?

14. Which musical's characters include Miss Honey and Miss Trunchbull?

15. Which musical's offerings include a line of fetish footwear for transvestite's

16. Which Rodgers and Hammerstein stage show includes the song 'Now Is the Time' which was cut from 'South Pacific'?

17. Which rock duo wrote the score for 'Spider-Man: Turn off the Dark'?

18. Which musical came to Broadway in 2011 with Whoopi Goldberg as lead producer?

19. Whose songs feature in 'Anything Goes'?

20. Which musical finds a novel use for ping-pong balls to the sound of M's 'Pop Muzik'?

. . . .

1. Which poet wrote detective novels under the pseudonym Nicholas Blake?

2. Blanchette was the original name of the colourful heroine in which fairy story?

3. What is the three-letter name of Bruce Wayne's dog in Batman comic strips?

4. What is Salman Rushdie's first name?

5. What is high-flying Colonel Kurt Steiner's codename in 'The Eagle Has Landed'?

6. What is the literary significance of 28 years, two months and 19 days?

7. At what age do Hobbits become adults?

8. Which writer is credited with writing between 37 and 54 plays?

9. Which movie is based on Walter Wager's thriller novel '58 Minutes'?

10. Which author is the unseen narrator of the 1945 movie adaptation of his own play 'Blithe Spirit'?

11. What is the name of the 'Captain Pugwash' cabin boy?

12. Which fictional traveller lived at No 7, Saville Row, Burlington Gardens, the house in which Sheridan died?

13. Which novel that became a much-loved movie begins, 'I'm always drawn back to the places where I lived, the houses and their neighbourhoods'?

14. At the start of a very famous novel, who is described as, 'Not beautiful'?

15. Which fictional setting for a novel that became a musical will you find if you, 'ask the policeman at the crossroads'?

16. Which month is it at the start of Orwell's '1984'?

17. What is Indian Summer like, according to Grace Metalious' novel 'Peyton Place'?

18. What was Robinson Crusoe's home city?

19. With what does E.B. White compare the size of newly-born Stuart Little?

20. Which is Robert Cohn's sport in Hemingway's 'The Sun Always Rises'?

1. In which city is the museum displaying 'The Red Vineyard', the only one of his own paintings sold by Vincent van Gogh?

2. What does the description 'plein air' tell you about a painting?

3. Which word describes the green colouration that develops on bronze sculptures?

4. What was the original intended setting for an icon?

5. What did Aldous Huxley describe as: 'A mixture of greenhouse and hospital ward, furnished in the style of a dentist's operating chamber'?

6. What did Andy Warhol claim two people kissing always look like?

7. Which High Renaissance megastar began his art career forging ancient Roman statues?

8. What was Degas' first name?

9. Which conflict was just beginning as Art Nouveau came to an end?

10. What name did Jackson Pollock give to his splashing and dripping technique?

11. Which fluid do artists usually use to thin acrylic paint?

12. Which industry made the fortune used by Samuel Courtauld to sponsor the arts?

13. Which world-renowned artist was jailed twice in his teens for shoplifting?

14. For which city's cathedral was Donatello's life-size statue of David intended?

15. Which famed American abstract impressionist bled to death after slashing his own arms?

16. Whose painting of 'The Lovers' depicts two people kissing with grey bags covering their heads?

17. Which of Hitler's henchmen bought a forged Vermeer painting he thought was genuine with half a million dollars he knew was forged?

18. Which part of the anatomy of a statue of St Peter in Rome is gradually being worn away by pilgrims' kisses?

19. Which medical condition is given as an explanation for the redish tint on some of Monet's paintings?

20. Which city's tourist attractions include the Rembrandt House?

1. What is Camp North Star's up-market rival in 'Meatballs'?

2. Al Pacino plays Big Boy Caprice in which movie?

3. What is the name of the Basset Hound on which Prof Sherman performs age-reversal experiments in 'Nutty Professor II'?

4. Which movie duo have the surnames Burns and Albright?

5. Which movie's opening scenes feature a Shanghai night-spot called Club Obi-Wan?

6. What is the name of the club owned by Goldmember in the movie 'Austin Powers in Goldmember'?

7. What are Cindy and Sandy in 'Jaws - 3D'?

8. What are the movie-inspired names of the kidnapped billionaire's animated bodyguards in 'Diamonds Are Forever'?

9. Which movie sees Danny DeVito's character hiding out in a defunct zoo exhibit titled 'Arctic World'?

10. Which movie sees Marilyn Monroe advertising Dazzledent toothpaste?

11. What is the appropriate title of the newspaper in 'Dick Tracy'?

12. In which of his movies does Elvis play Vince Everett?

13. For how many years was the Genie trapped in the lamp in Disney's 'Aladdin'?

14. What is Edmund Gwenn's seasonal role in a classic 1947 movie?

15. What is the name of the motorcycle gang who chase Beddoe in 'Any Which Way You Can'?

16. What is the name of the 'Police Academy' biker bar?

17. What is the colourful name of Cool Hand Luke's pet dog?

18. In the Austin Powers movies what does Dr Evil call his cat?

19. How many teeth has Disney's Goofy?

20. What does Arnie steal from the Alamo Sports Shop in 'The Terminator'?

1. Who have a sign on their fence reading 'Beware of The Thing'?
2. What is measured in Orkan Bleems on 'Mork and Mindy'?
3. What was Blitzen, Radar O'Riley's pet on 'M*A*S*H'?
4. What is the name of Mr Spock's mommy?
5. '45 Minutes From Harlem' was the working title for which long-running sitcom?
6. Which member of the Fly Girls dance group in the series 'In Living Color' went on to superstardom?
7. Who commands the Starship Swinetrek in the 'Muppet Show' 'Pigs in Space' sketches?
8. Which member of the 'Happy Days' cast was a founder of the Imagine Entertainment movie company?
9. What is the Alma Mater of Peg and Al in 'Married ... With Children'?
10. What is the first name of Bart Simpson's school teacher Miss Krabappel?
11. Which fast food restaurant employs SpongeBob SquarePants?
12. What is the name of the resident bloodhound on 'King of the Hill'?
13. What is Carla Tortilla's maiden name on 'Cheers'?
14. Who is Hong Kong Phooey's janitor alter ego?
15. Which TV family frequent the Rusty Barnacle seafood restaurant?
16. What is sold by the store that's a front for Tony's illegal operations on 'The Sopranos'?
17. What is the geographical link between 'The Simpsons', 'The Guiding Light' and 'Father Knows Best'?
18. What is Peg Bundy's somewhat unfortunate maiden name on 'Married ... With Children'?
19. With whom does Xander Harris house share in 'Buffet the Vampire Slayer'?
20. What is the name of the 'Family Guy' dog?

1. Which bodily orifice can be afflicted by an excess of cerumen?

2. How many biscupids are to be found in a full set of adult teeth?

3. Which disease takes its name from Greek words meaning 'joint' and 'inflamation'?

4. What are lubricated by lacrimal fluid?

5. Which organ can be affected by glossitis?

6. What is the common name for herpes labialis?

7. What does someone described as a bibliosmiac enjoy the smell of?

8. What did Greek physician Hippocrates say flowed through the veins?

9. What percentage of oxygen entering your blood stream is used by the brain?

10. What is the common, five-letter, name for urticaria?

11. What do people usually rush to find when they experience a gastrocolic reflex?

12. What is used in fango therapy?

13. What lie immediately below the adrenal glands?

14. What are there approximately half a million of on the average human foot?

15. When do human teeth start growing?

16. In 1976, what was Ray Brennan the first person to be killed by?

17. What is the common name for pediculosis?

18. Which complaint was once known as 'school sores'?

19. What is the alternative name for the third molar?

20. Which month sees the highest number of births in the U.K. and U.S.?

1. Which creatures does a cynophobic fear?

2. Which part of a firefly's anatomy flashes?

3. What are Georgia Jumpers and Night Crawlers?

4. How regularly does the average penguin have sex?

5. What is causing the most damage to the Great Barrier Reef?

6. Which river is home to the largest percentage of the world's electric eels?

7. What does the desert-dwelling addax antelope virtually survive without that is essential for other animals?

8. Which fish family's only entirely freshwater dweller is the burbot?

9. What is the main natural source of alginates?

10. Which is the world's largest web-footed bird?

11. What is the praying mantis the only insect to get through life with only one of?

12. What is the collective name for a group of budgerigars?

13. Which creature's ivory is called ribazuba?

14. Which is the first bird name checked in the Bible?

15. What type of creature is a goosander?

16. How many chambers has a fish's heart?

17. How many petals has a buttercup?

18. How many feet has a snail?

19. Other than humans, what species includes muggers?

20. How many legs has a scorpion?

1. In which month can you look up and see the Wolf Moon?

2. What was Pythagoras's theory when it came to putting his clothes on?

3. Which decade saw the first nylon stockings?

4. In 1947, what was Kenneth Arnold the first to report seeing?

5. Which decade saw the first Atlantic crossing by a jet aircraft?

6. For which branch of science were the Chaldeans famed?

7. Which Apollo mission was the final rehearsal for the first manned Moon landing?

8. During which century did mathematicians first use plus and minus signs?

9. What word describes things floating in the sea?

10. Which war saw the first attack with a bazooka?

11. What was the nationality of Nicolas Copernicus?

12. What fuel did Leonardo da Vinci use in his first high-intensity lamps?

13. How many sides has an icosahedron?

14. Which decade saw the first crewless radio-controlled flight from the U.S. to the U.K.?

15. What have you probably got in your pocket right now that was invented in 1950 by Frank McNamara?

16. In which decade did Britain's first airship make its maiden flight?

17. Which nation invented a chewing gum that monitors stress according to colour change?

18. Which decade witnessed the first colour TV transmission?

19. What stand on caisons?

20. Which military vehicle did Ernest Swinton claim to be co-inventor of?

. . . .

1. Who sued 'Hard Copy' magazine for claiming he'd moved to Atlanta to be close to an AIDS clinic?

2. Which rock star is the subject of the book 'Simply Mick'?

3. How did explorer Roald Amundsen die?

4. Who advised Theresa May to sue the European Union?

5. What is the surname of the 19th century Parisian tyre manufacturer with the first name Andre?

6. Which nature-loving U.S. President said of trees: 'When you've see one Redwood, you've seen them all'?

7. Which English actor shared a house dubbed 'Cirrhosis-by-the-Sea' with Errol Flynn?

8. Who was known as the Wizard of Menlo Park?

9. Which pop and film star's mother was the eldest child of Nobel Prize-winning nuclear scientist Max Born?

10. Which Brit band's Woodstock performance was interrupted by social activist Abbie Hoffman?

11. How many children had Paul McCartney fathered up to the start of 2017?

12. What nationality is porn star and politician Cicciolina?

13. What did 16th century prophet Nostradamus gaze into while making his predictions?

14. Who did Warren Beaty refer to as: 'A big, beautiful, generous fact of life we should all relax and enjoy'?

15. In which city did Elvis die?

16. Which member of the Apollo 11 crew once made a living making donuts?

17. Which wife did John Derek slot in between Ursula Andress and Bo Derek?

18. Who said his epitaph should read: 'Born, died, bit the heads off things'?

19. What did psychoanalyst Sigmund Freud confess to doing twenty times each day?

20. From which iconic attraction did actress Lillian Millicent Entwistle jump to commit suicide?

. . . .

1. Which English habit is first recorded in Pepys' diary on September 25th 1660?

2. In which city do Mormons expect the City of God to be built?

3. What is a felucca?

4. Which religion has a secret language called Pali?

5. What is the proper name for the prongs of a fork?

6. What is the English name for a place the Japanese know by the English phrase, 'Hello Work'?

7. What type of production is Copeland's 'Billy the Kid'?

8. What begins on Ash Wednesday?

9. What is the English meaning of the Spanish phrase; 'Que sera sera'?

10. At what time does tradition say April 1st tricks should end in Britain?

11. In which direction should the head of the deceased point at a Japanese funeral?

12. What job do Fluffers do on the London Underground?

13. Whose portrait graced the world's first adhesive postage stamp?

14. What creatures did ancient Egyptians think Bast was the mother of?

15. How many stars were on the Star Spangled Banner when 'The Star Spangled Banner' was written?

16. Which sign of the zodiac is the first air sign of the calendar year?

17. What does an old Turkish proverb say should be, 'Black as hell, strong as death and as sweet as love'?

18. Which is the only crime defined in the U.S. Constitution?

19. What does a gecko possess that all other lizards lack?

20. Which was the first song sung in outer space?

. . . .

1. Why was Greek huntsman Acteon turned into a stag and eaten by his own dogs?

2. What was 30 tonnes of Lithuania's temporary currency turned into in 1994?

3. How many hours should you put your watch back if you fly from London to New York to do your Christmas shopping?

4. What did Moses view from Mount Nebo?

5. Which of a ship's three masts is called the mizzen; front, middle or rear?

6. Which country had the first Y.M.C.A.?

7. What are Macgillycuddy Reeks?

8. What pre-flight essential for many travellers was first seen at Shannon Airport in Ireland?

9. What is celebrated seven days before Easter Sunday in most Christian countries?

10. Which name is shared by English pubs displaying Richard II's badge on their sign?

11. What were first displayed on a British car in 1935?

12. Which country's drivers have the international registration letters IL?

13. How many road wheels has a tuk tuk?

14. Which letter did Don Diego de la Vega scratch on walls?

15. What does the Sixth Commandment tell you not to do?

16. Which country sent Britain its first supply of frozen meat in 1880?

17. What was London's Savoy Theatre the first in the world to boast?

18. Into what is the Japanese Yen divided?

19. What name is given to English pubs displaying Henry VIII's badge on their sign?

20. How many children had Adam and Eve for their parents?

. . . .

1. What is the minimum number of letters permitted in a first Scrabble word?

2. What is the lowest score it is impossible to make with one dart?

3. Which modern casino game was known as Hazard in the 18th century?

4. What is the total of the hidden spots if three dice are stacked with a four visible on top?

5. What are you playing if you decline a Queen's Gambit?

6. What are measured on the Elo Scale?

7. Which game was issued in a waterproof version in 1967 for those who liked to play in their swimming pool?

8. Which pub game is Danny playing when he first sees the Grady Daughters in 'The Shining'?

9. Which game gave rise to the saying 'knuckle down'?

10. What were part of the original Battleships game that have now been taken out?

11. Which boxed game was the first non-drink or food product sold by Starbucks?

12. Which game takes its name from a Swahili word meaning 'to build'?

13. Who is Jake the Jailbird?

14. Which other game gives its name to using all your Scrabble tiles in one go?

15. Which is the favoured metal for competition darts?

16. Which planet is the space marine sent to when he assaults the commanding officer in the game Doom?

17. Which is the lowest scoring snooker ball after red?

18. What is the central division of a backgammon board called?

19. In which pub game do you get to peg-out?

20. Which company produced the 64-bit 'Jaguar' game?

1. Which Biblical city's name means 'House of bread'?

2. Which capital city is served by Bole International Airport?

3. What is the capital and largest city in Afghanistan?

4. Which country's seat of government is in Cotonou?

5. How many stars decorate the flag of Burundi?

6. Malo, Fogo and Brava are parts of which archipelago?

7. Which country is joined to Chile on its shortest land border?

8. How many major river systems flow through China?

9. In which country does the Orinoco start its flow?

10. Which country has Nicaragua to its north and Panama to its south?

11. Which island is the westernmost of the West Indies?

12. Which British city is the home of the Loiners?

13. Which nation's landscape is dominated by the Bohemian Massif?

14. Which is the smallest of the Scandinavian countries?

15. Which country occupies the Jutland Peninsula?

16. Which country's capital, Santo Domingo, is the oldest, still occupied, European settlement in the Americas?

17. Which is the only European capital city on the Atlantic Ocean?

18. What is the main religion of East Timor?

19. What colour is the bottom stripe on the flag of Egypt?

20. What is at the centre of the coat of arms on the flag of Equatorial Guinea?

1. Who was America's first incumbent President to survive being shot?

2. Which country declared war on the Allies and also on Germany in World War II?

3. What was Chiang Kai-Shek's snacky codename with the Allies in World War II?

4. What was the Bounty's main cargo when the famed mutiny took place?

5. On which nation's soil was the first battle involving tanks fought?

6. Who sailed for almost three years to become the first Englishman to circumnavigate the globe?

7. Which country's Civil War has been described as the rehearsal for World War II?

8. Which country was secretly invaded by the U.S. in 1970?

9. Which was the host city for the first U.N. General Assembly?

10. Which Tsar gave his support to Rasputin?

11. Who informed the world: 'He who holds Paris holds France'?

12. From which country did Tunisia, Morocco and Algeria all fight to gain independence?

13. Which of the famed beaches witnessed the heaviest resistance on D-Day?

14. Which product did Nikita Kruschev claim saved the starving Russian Army in World War II?

15. Which country suffered the most combat casualties in World War II?

16. Which body of water was the Spanish Armada trying to secure when it was defeated in 1588?

17. What was David Livingstone doing when he died?

18. Which TV character's name came from a man who investigated Al Capone?

19. Which birthday did Louis XIV of France celebrate five weeks after his coronation?

20. Who was the first serving U.S. President to visit Moscow?

- -

1. Which rock star's perfume collection includes 'Meow!' and 'Killer Queen'?

2. Which of the four main fashion weeks comes last?

3. What did Ernest Beaux create in 1920 that has been acknowledged as the most popular perfume on the planet?

4. Which fashion icon's tattoos include an M&Ms character and SpongeBob SquarePants?

5. Which fashion statements were originally fashioned from old car tyres?

6. What did Christian Louboutin create to give brides that 'something blue,' only seen if the couple kneel to pray?

7. Which fashion icon was ranked 12th on OUT magazine's list of the world's most powerful gay men and women?

8. Which are the two most important flowers in the perfume industry?

9. Where on the body do experts say perfume should be applied for the best results?

10. Who produce 'Tuscany' fragrance for men?

11. Which city is the home of 'Aramis'?

12. With what do Gieves and Hawkes of Savile Row supply discerning men?

13. Which fashion house claims, 'Style goes beyond time'?

14. Which artist's name follows 'Paloma' in the name of a perfume?

15. Which famous actress launched 'Passion' perfume in 1988?

16. Who advertised that a perfume should be 'a work of art'?

17. Whose fragrance range includes 'Jazz'?

18. What is the first name of shirt maker Mr Pink?

19. Which lingerie brand was launched by Michelle Mone who, in 2015, became Baroness Mone of Mayfair?

20. Who boasted: 'Style is never out of fashion.

1. Which Elvis song became the U.K.'s 1000th chart-topper when re-released in 2005?

2. What was the name of Bob Marley's female backing trio?

3. Who wrote the lyrics for 'Rocket Man' and 'Your Song'?

4. Whose second album included the hits 'Hot In Herre' and 'Dilemma'?

5. Who was the best-selling female artist in the U.S. in the 2000s?

6. Whose 'Empire State of Mind' collaboration with Jay Z spent a month atop the U.S. Billboard chart?

7. Whose second album was the Spanish language 'Mi Reflego' and third 'My Kind of Christmas'?

8. Which Australian pop duo consists of Darren Hayes and Daniel Jones?

9. What was the appropriate title of AC/DC's first album?

10. Which major music artist's death coincided with the 2012 Grammy Awards?

11. Which band dropped Ian Stewart from their official line-up in 1963 but employed him as their pianist until his death in 1985?

12. Who is the better-known half of the Bad Meets Evil rap duo?

13. What is the three-letter title of U2's debut album?

14. What was Billy Joel's first hit single?

15. Which heavy rockers broke into the mainstream with their 'Toys in the Attic' album?

16. How many times have The Who topped the U.K. singles chart?

17. Which sport is showcased in Bruce Springsteen's 'Glory Days'?

18. Which Dire Straits collection was the first album to sell a million copies on CD?

19. Which band's 'St Anger' album is showcased in the movie 'Some Kind of Monster'?

20. Who became Mrs Shawn Cory Carter in 2008?

1. Who was the first American to collect three consecutive Wimbledon singles titles?

2. How many of his 61 fights did Muhammad Ali lose?

3. Which decade saw the first sub-four-minute mile?

4. Which body of water can be seen from the first tee at St Andrews?

5. Who beat Serena Williams in the 2018 Wimbledon Women's Singles final?

6. Which Scottish-born innovator built the boat that held the world water speed record in 1919?

7. Which Bond movie includes an appearance by tennis star Vijay Amritraj?

8. How many players take to the pitch for a game of Canadian Football?

9. Which item of sporting equipment has Indian Pendants?

10. How many furlongs are left to run if a horse is half way round a mile and a quarter track?

11. What did author Rudyard Kipling invent for those who like to play golf in the snow?

12. In what sports gear was Princess Diana photographed when her marriage was first rumoured to be on the rocks?

13. Who did Germany beat 1-0 in the 2014 World Cup final?

14. Who unexpectedly beat Italy to knock England out of the 2014 World Cup?

15. Which month saw the opening ceremony of the 2018 Winter Olympics?

16. What made Fred Baldasare's 1962 cross-Channel swim newsworthy?

17. Which sporting trophy has been dubbed 'the ugliest salad bowl in the world'?

18. Who was voted BBC Sports Personality of the Year in 2017?

19. Which anniversary did the London Marathon celebrate in 2011?

20. How many combinations of trebles bets can be made across four horses?

· ·

1. What is the four-letter title of the musical with the subtitle 'A Tribute to the Beatles on Broadway'?

2. Which 2012 musical adaptation of 'The Apartment' is a showcase for the music of Bacharach and David?

3. 'American Idiot' features the music of which rock band?

4. Which musical features a drag queen called Albin?

5. Catherine Zeta-Jones made her Broadway debut alongside Angela Lansbury in the 2009 revival of which classic musical?

6. Which city gives its name to the title of a musical that sees a guy called Louis land a job as a radio DJ?

7. Which musical, scored for a small rock combo, won the 2010 Pulitzer Prize for Best Drama?

8. Glam rock and heavy metal feature in which musical set on Sunset Strip in 1987?

9. Which 1960s musical was revived in 2009 and featured cast members scattering flower petals and braiding the hair of audience members?

10. Which is the musical if Maria is unaware that her boyfriend has killed her brother in a knife fight?

11. Which stage musical hears the recorded voice of Julie Andrews asking patrons to turn off their phones before the curtain rises?

12. Which musical, set in County Durham, rotates three young actors in the lead role?

13. Which musical's sets include a 3-D animation of a painting by Seurat?

14. Which stage musical's actors wore sneakers with wheels in the heels so they looked to be floating?

15. Which 2007 revival included extra songs written by John Farrar and Barry Gibb?

16. What was Mel Brooks' Broadway follow-up to 'The Producers'?

17. Which musical is based on a novel by Amanda Brown that became a movie starring Reese Witherspoon?

18. Which musical includes Phil Collins' song 'You'll Be In My Heart'?

19. Tina Turner, Cindy Lauper and Nancy Reagan have all been impersonated in which musical?

20. What is the name of the fifth character in the title of Willy Russell's musical about the Beatles and the name of the chimney sweep in 'Mary Poppins'?

1. Which South Korean county hosted the first Winter Olympics to see bob sled competitors from five continents?

2. What were the 1908 London Olympics the first to provide for swimming competitors?

3. In 1912, which became the first Asian nation to compete in the Olympics?

4. Which year saw the first Olympics contested by five continents?

5. What was first heard at the 1920 Olympics?

6. Which was the first city to stage the Modern Olympics twice?

7. What became conventional after being introduced to runners in the 1928 Amsterdam Olympic stadium?

8. What had Swedish pentathlete Hans-Grunner Liljenwall taken resulting in the first Olympic drugs disqualification?

9. What was Norma Enriqueta Basillo's Olympic first in 1968?

10. At the 1972 Munich Games, what breed of dog was Waldi, the first Olympic mascot?

11. Which year saw Moscow host the first games in a communist country?

12. Who was the first athlete to light the flame then go on to win a gold medal?

13. For which country did Abebe Bikila run a barefoot marathon to become the first black gold medal winner?

14. In 1960, which city staged the first Olympics to be televised worldwide?

15. Which was the first city to host the Summer and Winter Olympics?

16. Who was the first athlete to win six Olympic sprint gold medals?

17. For which nation did gymnast Nadia Comaneci score the first Olympic perfect ten?

18. What did soccer referees first use in the 1968 Olympics?

19. In 1956, in which city were the first Games outside the U.S. or Europe held?

20. Which year first saw women competing in an Olympic Games at Olympia?

1. Which Sinclair Lewis novel begins: 'The towers of Zenith aspired above the morning mist'?

2. 'It was a queer sultry summer, the summer they electrocuted the Rosenbergs', are the opening words of which book by a woman writer?

3. Aldous Huxley begins which novel with: 'A squat gray building of only thirty four storeys'?

4. Which novel that became a much-loved movie begins: 'On the morning of August 8, 1965, Robert Kincaid locked the door of his small, two room apartment'?

5. At the start of 'Call of the Wild', what do we learn that Buck didn't read?

6. Which of Voltaire's works begins in the country of Westphalia?

7. Which Stephen King novel's opening line is: 'Nobody was really surprised when it happened'?

8. Which J.D. Salinger classic begins: 'If you really want to hear about it, the first thing you'll probably want to know is where I was born ...'?

9. What romantic cliché provides the first six words of 'Catch-22'?

10. Which children's story begins: 'Where's Papa going with that axe'?

11. Whose death is reported in the first three words of 'A Christmas Carol'?

12. Which novel that became a movie with 11 Oscar nominations but no wins, begins: 'You'd better never tell nobody but God'?

13. What month is is at the start of Dostoevsky's 'Crime and Punishment'?

14. Hemingway begins which novel with: 'In the late summer of that year ...'?

15. What is the title of the Isaac Asimov novel if: 'His name was Gaal Doric and he was just a country boy ...'?

16. Which novel by a Bronte Sister begins: 'There was no possibility of taking a walk that day'?

17. Which novel's opening words are: 'Mike Bowman whistled cheerfully as he drove his Land Rover through the Cabo Blanco Biological Reserve'?

18. Which bestseller begins: 'Christmas won't be Christmas without any presents grumbled Jo, lying on the rug'?

19. Which river is name checked in the first line of 'Rip Van Winkle'?

20. Who is the first animal named in 'Wind in the Willows'?

• •

1. How many fingers does Alien have on each hand?

2. Which cartoon character has always been 34-years-old?

3. Why is the number 75 significant for Forrest Gump?

4. In 'Our Man Flint' what does Flint own that has 83 different functions?

5. What is the name of the occult bookstore in 'Just Like Heaven'?

6. Who is the unseen, gun-loving, narrator of the 1998 movie 'Armageddon'?

7. Which movie star directed and narrated 'Duplex'?

8. Who is the Welsh-born narrator of 'When the Grinch Stole Christmas'?

9. Who met Vicki Vale at the Flugelhelm Museum?

10. Which escort agency features in 'L.A. Confidential'?

11. Who sings the backing vocals for Butterfly Boucher's rendition of the song 'Changes,' heard in 'Shrek 2'?

12. How many Oscars did 'La La Land' collect in 2017?

13. Which animated hero is given the honorary Indian name Flying Eagle?

14. Which James Bond villain has the legendary swimming pool full of sharks?

15. Which Hitchcock movie's clues include a cigarette lighter engraved 'From A to G'?

16. Which Disney movie includes a spell beginning 'Higitus Figitus'?

17. In which movie does Ringo call his girlfriend Honey Bunny?

18. In which movie is Heather Donahue seen with a book titled 'How to Stay Alive in the Woods'?

19. Which was second in the 'Indiana Jones' series?

20. What is the movie if Frankie Dunn hangs out at Ira's Roadside Diner?

. . . .

1. Who receives the most prank calls from Bart Simpson?

2. What is Buffy the Vampire Slayer's surname?

3. In 'The Big Bang Theory' what is Penny called by her dad?

4. Which popular U.S. TV series was remade in Spanish with the lead character renamed Walter Blanco?

5. How many sisters does Joey Tribbiani have on 'Friends'?

6. Who is the only unmarried main character on 'How I Met Your Mother'?

7. Which TV title character has a former girlfriend called Elaine Marie Benes?

8. Which city is the setting for 'The Wire'?

9. Which TV series features Nikolai's Flower Shop?

10. Which world famous 'Star Trek' fan talked Nichelle Nichols into staying on as Lt. Uhura when she planned to leave?

11. Which company made the piano owned by the Flintstones?

12. Which chat show star told the cast of 'Friends': 'I'd like to see y'all get a black friend'?

13. Which series' 2015 episodes included 'The Girl Who Died' and 'The Woman Who Lived'?

14. Which country ditched 'The Price is Right' when rampant inflation kept screwing up the answers?

15. Which sci-fi star was told to keep his mouth closed when he shared TV's first multi-racial kiss?

16. What colour is Papa Smurf's hat?

17. What is the name of the rich brat, missing and presumed dead, in 'Arrow'?

18. In which building did Olivia Pope work before setting up her crisis management company in 'Scandal'?

19. Which city provides the setting for 'Ripper Street'?

20. Which 2012 TV series had April living above a business called Second Time About?

• •

1. Which world-famous tourist attraction stands on the banks of the river Yamuna?

2. Which iconic structure has 294 steps from top to bottom?

3. How many vowels are there in the Hawaiian alphabet?

4. How many Commonwealth countries, other than Britain, include the British Union Flag on their own flag?

5. Caen is the capital of which French Department that shares its name with a drink?

6. Which is the world's most heavily-populated river basin?

7. Which is the only country bordering Brunei?

8. Which city's Hebrew name means Hill of Spring?

9. By what name is the former Idlewild Airport now known?

10. Which country's literary name is Innisfail?

11. Which volcano is dubbed the 'Lighthouse of the Mediterranean?

12. Lower Canada was the former name of which province?

13. Which island's tourist destinations include the beautiful Troodos Mountains?

14. What is the better-known name of the Naval Support Facility Thurmont?

15. Which river flows through Baghdad and Mosul?

16. Which volcanic island lies on the Sundra Strait between Java and Sumatra?

17. On which avenue does the French President review the annual 14th July parade?

18. Which is the most populace of New York's five boroughs?

19. Which group of holiday islands' main point of arrival is Lynden Pinding International Airport?

20. On which London building can shoppers see the motto 'Omnia Omnibus Ubique' (All things for all people everywhere)?

1. What colour are laburnum flowers?

2. What do sessile flowers lack?

3. Which is the main food of America's national bird the Bald Eagle?

4. What lets a crocodile mother know it's time to dig her newly hatched babies from the sand before they suffocate?

5. What is the 'Chinese ginkgo the oldest known surviving example of?

6. Which are the only big cats to live in family groups?

7. Which animal's milk, consumed by humans, does not curdle?

8. Which bird's varieties include macaroni, gentoo and chinstrap?

9. Which fruit can prove fatal to a parrot?

10. What does a cat have 32 of in each ear?

11. What colour is the blood of most insect species?

12. What percentage of a banana is fat?

13. Which geological period saw the arrival of the first dinosaurs?

14. How many non-retractable claws has a bear on each foot?

15. Of what does a butterfly have 380, a chicken 78 and a donkey 62?

16. What is the common name for a flower's corolla?

17. Which radio and TV term comes from an old word for scattering seeds?

18. What is the main food of adult echidnas?

19. When is the attractive scent of the plant oil petrichor most noticeable?

20. Something described as 'hircine' is related to which animal?

1. What does a spirometer measure?

2. Which is the most common colour of lapis lazuli?

3. Which science did Gregor Mendel develop in 1866?

4. What has been refined if you are left with bagasse pulp?

5. What did the Space Shuttle Challenger land in during September 1983 that it hadn't previously landed in?

6. What do most modern cruise ships use as ballast?

7. What does a mordant fix?

8. Which letter did Marconi continuously tap out in his first trans-Atlantic wireless transmission?

9. Which world first is claimed by the Somerset town of Chard?

10. Which three-letter title was given to the first Commodore home computer?

11. What is the common name for the soothing liquid hamamelis?

12. What is powdered then heated to produce enamel?

13. Which decade saw the first manned flight into the stratosphere?

14. Which was the first car company found to be cheating on emissions tests in 2015?

15. What fraction of sea-level air pressure exists at the summit of Mount Everest?

16. What were fifth generation iPods the first to offer?

17. What did the Pye record company introduce to hi-fi enthusiasts in 1958?

18. What is the surname of balloon travelling pioneers Joseph and Etienne?

19. What indicated the time on an ancient Egyptian clepsydra?

20. What was the Boeing 787 renamed in 2005?

. . . .

1. Which actor was the first well-known person to announce he was suffering from AIDS?

2. Who was the last King of France?

3. What nationality was Sigmund Freud?

4. Whose countless quips include; 'Will you marry me? Did he leave you any money? Answer the second question first'?

5. Which religious leader's father was named Abdallah?

6. Which murdered girl's name was used by British sailors as a nickname for canned meat?

7. What made J.D. Rockefeller his fortune?

8. Who was made the first honorary citizen of the U.S.A.?

9. Which King is said to have died due to injuries caused by the pommel of his saddle?

10. Which King Henry was Richard the Lionheart's father?

11. Which Nobel Prize was Wilhelm Roentgen the first to receive?

12. Whose excuse for sleeping with naked young girls was to prove he had the willpower not to touch them?

13. What did rock star Jim Morrison die just one day too early to celebrate in 1971?

14. Which store owner originated the phrase; 'The customer is always right'?

15. For what is the Amati family best remembered?

16. Which British monarch died in the same year Nobel Prizes were first awarded?

17. What did King Magnus III of Norway regularly wear that was considered eccentric?

18. Which of the Bronte Sister lived longest?

19. Which famed artist and writer claimed to have seen angels up a tree in Peckham Rye, London?

20. Which country's Kings include Manuel the Fortunate?

1. What does FPS stand for in the world of video gaming?

2. Which video game offered a $1 million prize to its first World Champion in 2013?

3. What overtook 'Space Invaders' to become the world's most popular arcade game in 1980?

4. Which movie-based game saw James Bond pursuing Sanchez?

5. What's the game if G is trying to repel Dr Curien?

6. Which award-winning game introduced Blobert from Blobonia?

7. What are players trying to reach in the 'Jurassic Park' video game?

8. What are players searching for in 'King's Quest 1'?

9. Which rock star appears on the screen when gamers reach the cinema in 'Labyrinth'?

10. Which Princess has to be rescued from Ganon by Link?

11. Which sport features in 'Midnight Club' and 'Midnight Madness'?

12. Which sea provides the setting for 'Monkey Island' games?

13. Which game gets called 'M.K' by its fans?

14. Which pet simulation game has versions including 'Chihuahua and his Friends' and 'Dachshund and his Friends'?

15. If Alis is setting out to revenge the death of her brother, Nero, what is the game?

16. Which role-playing series has editions released in pairs including Red and Blue, Gold and Silver and FireRed and LeafGreen?

17. What is the name of the wizard in 'Gauntlet'?

18. Which role-playing game claimed a record 20-million players by the start of 2006?

19. Which name is shared by the baddie in 'Who Framed Roger Rabbit?' a mountain in 'Lord of the Rings' and a video game series?

20. Which animals does Tarzan care for in the video game 'The Black Caldron'?

1. Which is the only New England state without a coastline?

2. In 2017, which became the UK's largest UNESCO Heritage Site?

3. Which was Spain's last dependency in the Western Hemisphere?

4. Why is Anguilla named after a Spanish word for 'eel'?

5. What is Czar Kolokol in the Kremlin?

6. Which river enters the Mediterranean at Aboukir Bay?

7. Which arm of the Mediterranean lies between Italy and the former Yugoslavia?

8. What is the capital of Catalonia?

9. Which group of holiday islands include Formentera?

10. The Land of the White Eagle is a nickname for which country?

11. Which country gives the name of 'levadas' to its irrigated agricultural terraces?

12. What is dubbed the Crocodile River?

13. What is the four-letter Spanish name for a flat-topped hill?

14. What is the alternative name for Hollywood's Sunset Boulevard?

15. Which London tourist attraction boasts the famous Whispering Gallery?

16. Which country is the home of the Dyaks?

17. Which German city's English Garden was founded by an American?

18. For what is the Italian city of Carrara famed?

19. Which country can be reached from Italy via the Grand St Bernard Tunnel?

20. Which letter is in the name of every Australian state other than Victoria?

1. Which Vietnamese village will be forever remembered for William Calley's massacre?

2. What was Field Marshall Montgomery talking about when he said: 'That sort of thing might be tolerated in France but we're British'?

3. Which Japanese city was flattened by an earthquake in 1995?

4. Who was the first reigning British monarch to visit the U.S.A.?

5. Which tribe was led by Cochise?

6. What did 400 camels carry for well-educated 10th century Grand Vizier of Persia Badul Kassel?

7. Over which ocean did Amelia Earhart disappear?

8. Which freak weather killed 92 people in Bangladesh on April 14, 1986?

9. Which country owned Argentina prior to its independence in 1816?

10. In 1860, what was marine John Dalliger the last British sailor to suffer?

11. Which annual festival was being celebrated on the day Abraham Lincoln was assassinated?

12. Prior to his assassination in 1958, which country was ruled by King Faisal?

13. The Westphalia treaty ended which lengthy war?

14. In 1894, which European city became the world's first inland port?

15. Which day of the week in 1905 saw 500 strikers shot dead in St Petersburg?

16. Who remained alone in prison when Speer and von Schirach were released in 1966?

17. Which country went to war with Russia to kick off the Crimean hostilities?

18. For what crime was Marie Antoinette executed?

19. Which annual celebration is Anna Jarvis of Philadelphia given the credit for creating?

20. Which city's name was painted beneath that of the Titanic?

. . . .

1. Which colour toilet paper became trendy in 2005 when launched by the Portuguese Renova company?

2. Which fashion statement was banned from the Ascot royal enclosure in 1971?

3. Which fashion house owns the Maxim's restaurant brand?

4. Which actress bought the film rights to the story of Coco Chanel?

5. Which three words were printed on 1984's biggest selling rock-related T-shirt?

6. Who launched the 'Anglomania' collection?

7. What were usually hidden until Geoffrey Beene introduced them as a fashion statement in his 1999 Spring/Summer collection?

8. Who joined Elton John to sing the 23rd Psalm at Gianni Versace's funeral?

9. What is the native language of Furbies?

10. Which company announced in 1999 it was closing half its North American factories due to a slump in sales of its main product?

11. What brought complaints about John Galliano's 1999 Autumn/Winter collection?

12. Which city did Paco Rabanne flee from after hearing it would be destroyed when the Mir space station crashed back to Earth?

13. With which company did Claudia Schiffer sign a $10 million deal in 1992?

14. What is the name of John Galliano's off-the-peg range launched in 1991?

15. Which three-quarter length skin-tight pants take their name from an Italian island?

16. Who is by far the world's most famous user of Bronnley 'English Fern' soap and Cyclax 'Rose-Pink' lipstick?

17. In which store was Winona Ryder caught shoplifting?

18. Which fashion house designed uniforms for the Italian Army?

19. Who is credited with introducing polo shirts as a fashion item?

20. Whose fragrances are promoted by Christy Turlington?

1. To which city does Chivas Regal whisky trace its roots?

2. How many chefs' hats represent the highest Gault-Millau award for cooking?

3. Which country gave the world tacos?

4. Which country's soft drinks include cool cans of Mucos?

5. What are Vezzena and Vivaro?

6. Hybla honey comes from which Mediterranean island?

7. Which country brewed the first Tuborg?

8. What is 'pollo' on an Italian menu?

9. Which German city gave the world Beck's beer?

10. Which French region produces Medoc and St Emilion wines?

11. Bubbly-Jock is the Scottish name for which seasonal dish?

12. What is Chinese Tsing Tao?

13. What is the Indian equivalent of a kaen phed in Thailand?

14. Which country produces Fockink gin?

15. Beyonce, Pink and Britney all donned gladiatorial garb to advertise what?

16. What advertised itself as 'the world's most popular beer' at the start of the 21st century?

17. Which fish is on the ingredients list of Worcestershire Sauce?

18. For which sweet treat is the French town of Montelimar best known?

19. What gives the Italian liqueur Strega its distinctive golden colour?

20. Which other alcoholic drink is added to white rum to produce a Fluffy Duck cocktail?

. . . .

1. From which band did Richie Sambora split in 2013?

2. Which Abba single was released to commemorate 1979 as the International Year of the Child?

3. What is the stage name of Michael Ebenezer Kwadjo Omari Owuo Jr, a 2019 Glastonbury headliner?

4. Who are dubbed 'the most dangerous band in the world'?

5. Whose numerous alternative names included Jamie Starr and Joey Coco?

6. Which band tragically lost Danny Federici in 2008 and Clarence Clemons in 2011?

7. Who worked on Jay Z's 'Blueprint' album before launching his own hugely successful career with 'The College Dropout'?

8. Who was the most-played artist on British radio in the period 1984-2004?

9. Which British heavy-metal band's 'Bringing on the Heartbreak' was one of the first rock tracks screened on MTV?

10. What number was a chart hit title for Ellie Goulding in 2019?

11. In a 2012 obituary, who did the Times call : 'The undisputed Queen of the 70s disco boom'?

12. How many Wilson brothers were there in the original Beach Boys?

13. Who was lead singer with the Love Unlimited Orchestra?

14. In 2015, who was the first artist to win a U.S. Songwriter's Hall of Fame award for 'attaining iconic status in pop culture'?

15. What is Peter Gene Hernandez's stage name?

16. What is the subtitle of Meat Loaf's 'Bat Out of Hell III'?

17. Which of the Travelling Wilbury's dubbed himself Charlie T. Wilbury Jr.?

18. Which alternative hip-hop group included apl.de.ap, Tabbo, Fergie and will.I.am?

19. Who briefly renamed himself Makaveli?

20. How many full-length studio albums did Nirvana release in their seven-year career?

1. From what material are Kendo sticks manufactured?
2. In which decade did golfers first compete for the U.S. Masters?
3. For which sport is the Harmsworth Trophy a prize?
4. Who receives the Lev Yashin Award?
5. What colour is the outer scoring ring on an archery target?
6. What was Prince William hit on the head with in 1991, resulting in a reported fractured skull?
7. Which company's soccer shoes were promoted with the slogan: 'Leave your mark on a game'?
8. Which sport awards the Iran Cup and the Bride's Vase?
9. What interval in play was first added to the rules of cricket in 1892?
10. Which sport's equipment once included a feathery?
11. Which handicap mechanism in the rules of croquet and real tennis can also be a soup?
12. In 2015, who became a third-time winner of the Formula One world drivers' championship?
13. In 2015, which country won the tennis Davis Cup for the first time in 70 years?
14. Which sport's leading player is awarded the Balon d'Or?
15. Which sport's rules are controlled jointly by the R&A and the USGA?
16. What is your score on the chalkboard if you've just won a game of darts?
17. Who was the first woman with tennis earnings in excess of $21 million?
18. Which World Series has been won by the appropriately named Chris Moneymaker?
19. What's your sport if you compete for the Air Canada Silver Broom?
20. What percentage of the ball must cross the line to qualify for a football goal?

1. Which musical cast R&B diva Chaka Khan as Shug Avery?
2. 'Walk Like a Man' and 'Rag Doll' are just two of the songs in which jukebox musical?
3. Which musical is based on the Marlon Brando-David Niven movie, 'Bedtime Story'?
4. The origins of the Tin Man, Cowardly Lion and Scarecrow are explained in which musical?
5. Which musical is set where people and puppets live when they can't afford accommodation in Manhattan?
6. Which musical featuring Bob Dylan songs was seen as the follow-up to Billy Joel's 'Moving Out'?
7. Which titled British actor provided the recorded voice of the Giant for the 2002 re-launch of Sondheim's 'Into the Woods'?
8. What is the musical if chunky Tracy Tumblat sings 'Good Morning Baltimore', on her way to school?
9. Which musical features Donna, a former rock trio member, who now writes cookbooks?
10. Which city's public toilets see the start of the musical 'Urinetown'?
11. What is Nazi playwright Franz Leibkind's hobby in 'The Producers'?
12. What was the Musician's Unions' main complaint about the musical 'Contact'?
13. Elton John and Tim Rice wrote a musical that shares its name with which opera?
14. The revival of which Irving Berlin musical saw Reba McIntyre's Broadway debut?
15. What is the musical if dancing is forbidden within the city limits?
16. Which was the first Disney musical on Broadway?
17. Which song is reprised at the end of 'The Lion King'?
18. Which musical, based on a Robert Louis Stevenson novella, includes the songs 'No One Knows Who I Am' and 'Good 'n' Evil'?
19. For which musical did Julie Andrew reject a Tony nomination because she thought the whole cast should be nominated?
20. Which musical cheerfully opens with a corpse floating in a swimming pool?

. . . .

1. Which seasonal plaything was Neve, one of the mascots at the 2006 Turin Winter Olympics?

2. Which year saw the first Summer Olympics held entirely in the winter?

3. What name was given to the early New Zealand and Australia combined Olympic squad?

4. What is the Olympic sport of Jamie Hildebrand who officially changed his name to Kamikaze?

5. How many times had Botswana competed in the Winter Olympics up to and including 2018?

6. What was sold from their ship along the way to pay for 69 Brazilian athletes to attend the 1932 Olympics?

7. Why did the IOC expel Brunei from the 2008 Olympics?

8. What nickname was given to Equatorial Guinea's extremely slow swimmer at the Sydney Olympics?

9. Which European country added a crown on its flag after noticing at the 1936 Olympics that it was identical to the flag of Haiti?

10. Which country did tennis star Andre Agassi's father represent at the 1948 and 1952 Olympics?

11. Which country's 1912 Olympics included no boxing because it was against their law?

12. What were swimming in the pool that resulted in threats of a walkout by 1952 swimming contestants?

13. At which city's Games did Ray Leonard, Michael Spinks and Leon Spinks all win gold?

14. What were controversially sold for $3,000 prior to the 1984 Los Angeles Olympics?

15. Which players were banned from taking part when pro footballers were admitted to the Olympics in 1984?

16. For which sport did Dom Parsons win Britain's first medal at the 2018 Winter Olympics?

17. Under what name do the former U.S.-owned Caroline Islands now compete in the Olympics?

18. Which African country's only Olympic medals are four silvers won by sprinter Franke Fredericks?

19. Against whom did the U.S. basketball squad score a record 156 points at London 2012?

20. Which country had sent no female athletes to the Olympics prior to 2012 when four competed?

. . . .

1. What grooming items is Buck Milligan carrying at the start of James Joyce's 'Ulysses'?

2. Which novel's main character lives with Uncle Henry and Aunt Em?

3. Which famous fictional home was almost called Fontenoy Hall?

4. What is the misleading title of the third book in Isaac Asimov's 'Foundation Trilogy'?

5. Which John Steinbeck novella features an animal named Gabilan after a range of mountains?

6. What is Glimmerglass in James Fenimore Cooper's novel 'The Deerslayer'?

7. Which series' fourth book is titled 'So Long, and Thanks for All the Fish'?

8. Who wrote Hogwarts' first-year required reading book, 'A History of Magic'?

9. A famed radio adaptation of which novel began with an orchestra performing at the Hotel Park Plaza?

10. To what does Smee give the name Johnny Corkscrew in 'Peter Pan'?

11. What is Scarlett O'Hara's first name?

12. Which H Ryder Haggard novel is set in the city of Kor?

13. What does Minnehaha's name mean in Longfellow's 'The Song of Hiawatha?

14. Which book series includes 'The Prairie', 'The Pathfinder' and 'The Pioneers'?

15. Who invented lickable wallpaper?

16. Which book that became a popular movie has the subtitle 'A Life in the Woods'?

17. What kills Beth in 'Little Women'?

18. Which Dickens classic sees the law clerks hanging out at in inn called the Magpie and Stump?

19. Which comic book feline was born in Mamma Leoni's Italian restaurant?

20. In which novel is the most valuable substance in the universe a space travel essential called Melange?

1. What is the name of Ike Graham's cat in 'Runaway Bride'?

2. Which was Pierce Brosnan's first movie as James Bond?

3. Which desert-dwellers capture C-3PO and R2-D2 in 'Star Wars'?

4. What's the name of the pet mouse in 'Green Mile'?

5. Who are Jules and Verne in 'Back to the Future Part III'?

6. Which 2018 box-office smash sees T'Challa return home after the death of his father, the King of Wakanda?

7. In the movie 'Home Alone' what are the Kenosha Kickers?

8. Which capital city gave its name to the racehorse whose head is dumped in Jack Waltz's bed in 'The Godfather'?

9. What is Little Nellie in 'You Only Live Twice'?

10. In which movie does Tom Hanks' character work for the MacMillan Toy Company?

11. Which duo's many movies together include 'That's My Boy', 'Living It Up' and 'Artists and Models'?

12. Which name is shared by the dogs in 'The Little Mermaid' and 'How the Grinch Stole Christmas'?

13. Which English county gave its name to the town where 'Donnie Darko' is set?

14. Which movie character is the lead singer with a rock band called Ming Tea?

15. What is the name of Rocky's pet goldfish?

16. Which four-letter word appears in the title of five songs heard in 'An American Werewolf in London'?

17. Which Western begins with a caption reading; 'Most of what follows is true'?

18. Which mountain provides the setting for 'Drop Dead Gorgeous'?

19. In 'American Beauty', at which restaurant does Lester Turnham find a job after quitting as a writer?

20. Which Mel Brooks movie was hyped; 'Never give a saga an even break'?.

• •

1.   Which series is set in the fictional land of Westeros?

2.   Which TV title character uses a memory enhancement technique called Mind Palace?

3.   What is Corrado Soprano's nickname?

4.   Who had Homer Simpson just spoken to in London when he quipped: 'Wow! I can't believe we met Mr. Bean'?

5.   Which TV series spawned the 'Jesus v Satan' T-shirt?

6.   Who played the title character in the 1999 'Scarlet Pimpernel' TV series?

7.   How many puppies are in 'Paw Patrol'?

8.   What were the final four words on 'Cheers'?

9.   What did Candice Bergen's character become on 'Murphy Brown' to gain criticism from many U.S. politicians?

10. Which Telletubbie can speak Cantonese?

11. What was Joey's prize when he beat Rachel and Monica in a quiz on 'Friends'?

12. What's the TV series if special agent Dale Cooper investigates murder?

13. Which is the favoured restaurant with Moesha and her buddies?

14. Which 'Simpsons' character is the part-time lifeguard at a baptismal pool?

15. How many 'Friends' featured in the first series?

16. Which TV priest referred to the needy as: 'A shower of bastards'?

17. Whose 'Come Away With Me' album secured her the guest of honour gig on the 35th anniversary edition of 'Sesame Street'?

18. Which TV series is set mostly at 34 Claremont Avenue?

19. Which rock star played Leather Tuscadero, leader of a band called the Suedes, on 'Happy Days'?

20. What is the name of the annoyingly chatty cat on 'Sabrina the Teenage Witch'?

1. Which weather condition sees the most bee stings?

2. How many toes are there on each foot of a rhinoceros?

3. How many lungs has the average snake?

4. Which almost Biblical trick are Western Grebes the only birds capable of performing?

5. Which is the only truly amphibious member of the weasel family?

6. From what does a Fighting Fish construct its nest?

7. What is lacking from a sea creature categorised as agnatha?

8. What is a pochard?

9. What peculiarity gives a Portuguese Water Dog its name?

10. How many pairs of ribs has a cat?

11. What farm animal is known as a jumbuck to an Aborigine?

12. Which insect is mentioned 24 times in the Bible?

13. What colour stripe is down the centre of a natterjack toad's back?

14. What does an earthworm have five of but a human only one?

15. Which insect most commonly pollinates figs?

16. What does an average cat have one-hundred of but a dog only two?

17. What can a shark do with its eyes but no other fish can?

18. What does a bee have five of but a human only two?

19. Which animal cannot look up at the sky?

20. Which male mammals have the highest rate of homosexuality?

. . . .

1. Who became the only U.S. President with a patent when he invented a device to lift boats?

2. Which colour diamonds occur if nitrogen is present in their structure?

3. Which metal were the Chinese using in 300AD that the Western World didn't officially discover until 1827?

4. What did George Green patent in 1875 that, in a 2003 poll, was voted the second most-terrifying thing known to man after the nuclear bomb?

5. Which is the only metal that is naturally antibacterial?

6. Which is the densest-known stable element on earth?

7. How many noble metals are there?

8. Which was the first spacecraft to go there and back and then there and back again?

9. How many engines has a Boeing 737?

10. What is measured in angstroms?

11. Which country lies fourth on the 'most junk floating in space' chart?

12. Which name for calcium oxide can also be a citrus fruit?

13. What is Edward Teller known as the father of?

14. What are studied by limnologists?

15. Which number comes after 3.1 in pi?

16. Which metal is produced from cassiterite ore?

17. What are counted and measured on a cytrometer?

18. What do herpetologists study?

19. How many times brighter than a Half Moon is the Full Moon?

20. Which probe started sending pictures back from Mars in July 1997?

1. Whose mistress was Vlaretta Patacci?

2. What title is given to a scholar who studies the Marquis de Sade?

3. What type of vehicle did Prince Philip purchase to travel around in, in 1999?

4. What is a quidnunc eager to hear?

5. Which three-letter word means attempting to sell something under the guise of doing market research?

6. What name is given to the locks of hair worn at the side of the head by male Orthodox Jews?

7. Which title was Rana Raslan the first Arab to hold?

8. Which country did Prince Charles and Diana visit for their so-called 'second honeymoon' when they went off sailing on separate boats?

9. Who married singer Edie Brickell after a divorce from 'Star Wars' cutie Carrie Fisher?

10. Which Russian leader announced to the world that his mother knitted his socks?

11. Who was described by an Iraq newspaper as: 'A circus buffoon ... vomiting poison like a spotted serpent'?

12. Which former Spice Girl became a U.N. Goodwill Ambassador in 1998?

13. How many eyes did Lord Nelson have at the time of his death?

14. Who said of Courteney Cox: 'She smells like a truck driver and I like it'?

15. Which member of the British royal family was nicknamed 'Wombat' at school?

16. Who had a quote from the Beatles' song 'Sexie Sadie' tattooed on his arm for Sadie Frost?

17. Who was last seen at Twinwood Airfield, England, on December 15th, 1944?

18. Who said of a naked encounter with Madonna: 'She's going to say I couldn't, the truth is I wouldn't'?

19. Who reportedly told Princess Diana: 'I cannot imagine anyone in their right mind leaving you for Camilla'?

20. Which Welsh woman said she felt 'violated' when her wedding photos appeared in Hello! magazine?

• •

1. Which is the first city mentioned in the song 'Route 66'?
2. Which is the last city mentioned in the song 'Route 66'?
3. In which decade did the last section of Route 66 disappear from official maps?
4. In which decade was Route 66 commissioned to connect stretches of the existing road?
5. How many states were crossed by Route 66?
6. How many time zones were crossed by Route 66?
7. In which state was the shortest section of Route 66?
8. Which accepted alternative name for Route 66 was originally coined by John Steinbeck in his novel 'The Grapes of Wrath'?
9. What was the original purpose of the building in San Bernardino that is now the Route 66 Museum?
10. Which state boasts the exact centre of Route 66?
11. Which state had the most miles of the old Route 66?
12. Which city in the song 'Route 66' is the largest in the Texas panhandle?
13. Which city on Route 66 was known as the Helium Capital of the World?
14. Which town on Route 66 trotted to the top of the 2013 list naming America's most patriotic places?
15. Which city on Route 66 takes its name from something erected by a scouting party in 1876?
16. Which city in the song 'Route 66' is the home of the Lowell Observatory?
17. Which location in the song 'Route 66' is deliberately out of geographical order because its name rhymes with a state in the song?
18. Which town in the song 'Route 66' was once called Walnut?
19. In which city in the song 'Route 66' do the highways Route 66, Interstate 15, Interstate 40 and California State Route 58 all meet?
20. Which piano-playing singer had the first hit version of 'Route 66'?

Each of the following is worth two points. One point for naming the song from which the lyric is taken and another for naming the first artist or act to have a hit with this song either as a single or on an album.

1. 'I never wanted to be your weekend lover'
2. 'If I was a sculptor, but then again no'
3. 'I'm the new Sinatra, and since I made it here, I can make it anywhere'
4. 'Your smile is like a breath of spring. Your voice is soft like summer rain'
5. 'I want to feel sunlight on my face, see that dust cloud disappear without a trace'
6. 'I had to phone someone so I picked on you, hey that's far out so you heard him too'
7. 'Yes how many times must a man look up before he can see the sky?'
8. 'All I wanted to do was break your walls. All you every did was break me'
9. 'Through the mud and the beer, and the blood and the cheers, I've seen champions come and go'
10. 'I'm sitting here resting my bones, and this loneliness won't leave me alone'.
11. 'You held me down but I got up (hey!) already brushing off the dust'
12. 'No wedding Saturday within the month of June'
13. 'We only said goodbye with words. I died a hundred times'
14. 'Your skin so wet. Black lace on sweat'
15. 'We've been through this such a long long time, just trying to kill the pain'
16. 'Through these fields of destruction. Baptisms of fire'
17. 'And I hope you are having the time of your life. But think twice, that's my advice'
18. 'I'm a hot air balloon that could go into space, with the aim, like I don't care baby by the way'
19. 'I rode a tank held a general's rank when the blitzkrieg raged'
20. 'There's a sound outside the front door and I know it's just the wind'

1. Which member of U2 was once engaged to Naomi Campbell?

2. Whose best man speech at Liza Minnelli and David Gest's wedding ran to just seventeen words?

3. Who bought the ring in Aberystwyth then complained about the wedding photos?

4. In which country did Elvis first meet Priscilla?

5. Which star from the Bronx was the first person to win FHM magazine's Sexiest Woman in the World title twice in a row?

6. Who did Charles Dickens refer to as: 'A spot of blood and grease on the history of England'?

7. Which 42-year-old's wedding to toy boy Ashton Kutcher was attended by Bruce Willis who she had previously married twice?

8. What was Nigerian President Olusegun Obasanjo's vain wife doing in Marbella that led to her death?

9. Which was Nelson Mandella's favourite soup?

10. What is Barack Obama's middle name?

11. Which actor's real surname is Mapother?

12. Whom was Dr Conrad Murray convicted of the involuntary manslaughter of?

13. Which rock star collected statues of Joan of Arc?

14. Who married Ned Rocknroll in 2012?

15. Who married Nancy Shevell in 2011?

16. Who famously said Gerald Ford couldn't walk and chew gum at the same time?

17. What is Pixie Lott's first name?

18. Which former leader is godfather to one of Rupert Murdoch's children?

19. Who told Lennox Lewis: 'I wanna eat your heart, I wanna eat your children, praise be to Allah?

20. Who beat Princess Diana and Madonna into second and third place in the list of most-mentioned people in 1997 gossip columns?

1. In which city is the FBI headquarters?

2. Which country boasts the world's highest sand dunes?

3. What is the popular English name for Pamplona's Fiesta San Fermin?

4. Which is the commonest colour for European post boxes?

5. In Icelandic tradition, what must you purchase new for Christmas to avoid being eaten by the Yule Cat?

6. Which Persian Gulf state's name means 'Two Seas' in Arabic?

7. Which Australian city took its name from a small town in Derbyshire, England?

8. Which was the first country with an inter-city monorail system?

9. Which city must you visit if you are overcome with an uncontrollable desire to explore the Liberace Museum?

10. Prior to its independence, which county was Belgium a part of?

11. Which is Australia's westernmost city?

12. Which European country's flag is based on a blood-stained tunic?

13. Which Florida city takes its name from a Native American word for 'people of the peninsula'?

14. Which continent's name is based on a Roman word for 'sunny'?

15. Which country provides the biggest foreign tourist trade to Hawaii?

16. What was once known as Jabal Tariq, or, Mount Tariq?

17. Which country boasts the largest Spanish-speaking population?

18. Which south-westerly wind blows across France from Marseilles to Toulon mostly in the winter and the spring?

19. Which is the southernmost nation on the Balkan Peninsula?

20. Which country is home to the most Roman Catholics?

. . . .

1. Which European country ditched its monarchy in 1946?
2. How many U.S. Presidents were assassinated during the reign of Queen Victoria?
3. Which President of France died in office in 1974?
4. Which nation was dubbed 'The Meatball' during World War II?
5. Who went to bed with a poodle named Rufus Two?
6. Which Pacific island group did Japan attack the day after Pearl Harbor?
7. Which U.S. President claimed tax relief on underwear he'd donated to the Salvation Army?
8. Which European city saw 4,000 deaths due to killer fog in 1952?
9. In 1905, which nation did Japan defeat to establish itself as a major power?
10. What use did Ancient Egyptians find for a mixture of honey, sodium carbonate and crocodile dung?
11. Which was the first war to witness a jet plane shot down by another?
12. Why did people laugh when Abyssinian Emperor Menelik II said he would cut crime by buying electric chairs from the U.S.?
13. To whom did Idi Amin write: 'Your experience will be a lesson to all of us not to marry ladies in high positions'?
14. What did 16th century nun St Brigid serve as a drink to visitors at Kildare Abbey?
15. Who joined Ethelred the Unready and his bride in bed on their wedding night?
16. Who said of Ronald Reagan: 'He does not dye his hair, he's just prematurely orange'?
17. From which African country did Biafra break away?
18. Which London tourist attraction was originally intended as a gate for Buckingham Palace?
19. Which large island was claimed by Rome after the first Punic War?
20. What length of working week did the Polish Solidarity Movement strike for in 1981?

1. In 2013, what became the first dish made from lab-grown meat?

2. From which metal is the wire made that gives Gorgonzola cheese its blue veins?

3. Which cheese is most likely to be stamped 'Boerkenkass', Dutch for 'Farmer's cheese'?

4. What name is given to the counter between a restaurant kitchen and the waiting staff?

5. Which city's breweries include Hacker-Pschorr and Hofbrauhaus?

6. Which word completes Shirley Conran's observation: 'Life's too short to stuff a ...'?

7. Which chocolate manufacturer calls itself; 'the world's leading nutrition, health and wellness company'?

8. What is the surname of the German immigrant who introduced ready-made mayonnaise to New York in 1905?

9. Which fast-food chain came up with a sliced frankfurter sandwich called the Bender in a Bun?

10. Which fruit becomes the cheese accompaniment called membrillo?

11. Which fruit gives its flavour to Van Der Hum liqueur?

12. Which animal provides the milk for Serbian Pule Cheese, said to be the world's most expensive?

13. From what does the orange and champagne mix Buck's Fizz take its name?

14. What does 'Nam Chim' mean on a Thai menu?

15. Which country's national dishes include Pho noodle soup?

16. Which dish of barbecued lamb or chicken, served with tahini in pitta bread, is the Arabic equivalent of Turkey's doner kebab?

17. What is hollowed out then filled with curry to produce the South African dish known as Bunny Chow?

18. What is unique, but to purists unacceptable, about Mascarocofea vianneyi, Madagascan coffee?

19. What is found floating in a bottle of Mescal labelled 'con gusano'?

20. In what is a Japanese Bento meal traditionally served?

. . . .

1. Who sometimes went by the name Tuff Gong?

2. How many of the nine tracks on Michael Jackson's 'Thriller' were released as singles?

3. Name one of the two tracks from Pink Floyd's 'Dark Side of the Moon' that were released as A-sides on singles.

4. Which band's 'Back in Black' album is one of the world's top-ten best selling albums of all time?

5. Which album featuring Whitney Houston was the first ever to sell one million copies in a seven-day period?

6. Which Led Zeppelin album launched 'Stairway to Heaven'?

7. What was the world's biggest selling album in 1997?

8. Which Bruce Springsteen album became the first C.D. manufactured in the U.S. for commercial release?

9. Whose song 'Slippery When Wet' gave Bon Jovi an album title?

10. Which bonus track from 'Desperately Seeking Susan' was added to Madonna's 'Like a Virgin' album when it was re-released in 1985?

11. What is the opening track on U2's 'The Joshua Tree' album?

12. Which British royal probably thought he was complementing Bryan Adams when he told him: 'Your music vibrated my sternum'?

13. Whose 'All These Things That I've Done' ends with the totally meaningless: 'I've got soul but I'm not a soldier'?

14. Whose 'Independent Women Part 1' was a soundtrack single from 'Charlie's Angels'?

15. Which Kate Bush song became a dance floor hit for Futureheads?

16. Which band's rocking 'Plug In Baby' started life as a ballad?

17. Who was the other half of Gnarls Barclay along with producer Danger Mouse?

18. Which five-piece Brit band enjoyed worldwide success with 'One Day Like This'?

19. Who had 'Umbrella' turned down by her record company before it became a worldwide smash for Rihanna?

20. Which artist, known by a single name, topped charts worldwide in early 2018 with his song 'God's Plan'?

1. Which musical's characters include a dancing candelabra and teapot?

2. Which role did Elton John fill in the movie version of 'Tommy'?

3. With the opening of 'Miss Saigon' in 1991, who had five shows running simultaneously on Broadway?

4. Which musical reunited Andrew Lloyd Webber and Trevor Nunn for the first time since 'Starlight Express'?

5. Which massive musical was almost called 'Shut Up and Dance'?

6. What is Sir Galahad's first name in the musical 'Spamalot'?

7. Which country is the setting for the loco races in 'Starlight Express'?

8. Which former Spice Girl played Mary Magdalene in a 2013 revival of 'Jesus Christ Superstar'?

9. Which singer/songwriter is the subject of the musical 'Beautiful'?

10. 'Get Me To The Church On Time' is from which musical?

11. In 2012, what overtook 'The Phantom of the Opera' to become Broadway's top grossing show?

12. What is Julie Andrews holding in her left hand on the iconic 'Sound of Music' movie poster?

13. What is Adolf Hitler's middle name in 'The Producers'?

14. Which musical introduced the song 'You'll Never Walk Alone'?

15. Which Shakespeare play inspired 'West Side Story'?

16. Which musical tells the story of a group of young musicians and artists in Manhattan's lower East Side?

17. What is the name of the male flower shop assistant in 'Little Shop of Horrors'?

18. Which country provides the setting for 'Priscilla, Queen of the Desert'?

19. Which musical enthuses: 'What a glorious feeling, I'm happy again'?

20. Which musical introduced the song 'There's No Business Like Show Business'?

. . . .

1. Which game are you playing if you cross-wire your opponent's balls

2. At which sport was Idi Amin a Ugandan champion from 1951 to 1960?

3. Which European city supports the Grasshoppers soccer squad?

4. Which German city hosts the world's largest annual equestrian event?

5. Which annual sporting event is played for the Venus Rosewater Dish?

6. Which sport named a blocking move The Kong after King Kong's attempt to swat planes from the Empire State Building?

7. A donut is a goal scored by aiming at the keeper's head in which sport?

8. Which sport is said to have originated in the English village of Hambledon?

9. What is the English name for the sliotar, used in a game of hurling?

10. Which court game was once called Poona?

11. Who became the world's most expensive soccer player when he transferred from Juventus to Real Madrid for £47 million in 2001?

12. Which sport do women contest for the Uber Cup?

13. What is the alternative four-letter name for toboggan?

14. Which sport brought fame and fortune to 6ft 8in Chad Rowan, aka Akebono?

15. For whom did Mike Tyson purchase £1 million-worth of jewellery during a much publicised January 2000 London shopping spree?

16. In 1990, who became the first player ever expelled from the Australian Open tennis tournament?

17. Who was docked a point in the 1999 Australian Tennis Open when her hair beads spilled onto the court?

18. How many horse races comprise the English Classics?

19. Who lost his World Heavyweight title to Leon Spinks in 1978?

20. Who is the father of the baby born to Steffi Graf in 2001?

. . . .

1. What is the capital of Gondor in 'Lord of the Rings'?

2. What is David Caravaggio's code name in 'The English Patient'?

3. Which Herman Melville novel is subtitled 'A Narrative of Adventures in the South Seas'?

4. Emma Lazarus' poem 'The New Colossus' is carved into the base of which tourist attraction?

5. What is the capital of the underworld in John Milton's 'Paradise Lost'?

6. Which detective series includes 'The Case of the Caretaker's Cat' and 'The Case of the Lame Canary'?

7. What is Harry Angstrom's nickname in John Updike's series of books?

8. Which John Steinbeck novel was originally titled 'Salinas Valley'?

9. How many full-length Sherlock Holmes novels did Sir Arthur Conan Doyle write?

10. Which James M. Barrie character has the catchphrase 'Silly little ass'?

11. What does the drug Soma cause in Aldous Huxley's 'Brave New World'?

12. Which Rudyard Kipling novel is subtitled 'A Story of the Grand Banks'?

13. What is Templeton in E.B. White's book 'Charlotte's Web'?

14. What is the name of Dr Dolittle's pet owl?

15. What creature is Neville Longbottom's pet, Trevor, in the Harry Potter books?

16. Which Oscar Wilde work is subtitled 'A trivial comedy for serious people'?

17. How many years after the original is the sequel to 'The Three Musketeers' set?

18. Which Anna Rice series includes 'Blood and Gold', 'Blackwood Farm' and 'Blood Canticle'?

19. Which Ian Fleming novel was originally titled 'You Asked For It' when published in paperback in the U.S.?

20. For what is the Carnegie Medal awarded?

1. What is the name of the horse ridden by Casper, the Friendly Ghost?

2. Which 2005 film's closing credits include: 'No dragons were harmed in the making of this movie'?

3. Which movie stars Goldie Hawn as an actress appearing in a Broadway play titled 'Of a Certain Age'?

4. Which character plays the role of the Western villain, One-Eyed Bart, in 'Toy Story'?

5. What are orgas in the movie 'A.I. Artificial Intelligence'?

6. Which hotel hosts the title event in 'Bachelor Party'?

7. Peppering Eye village is the setting for which Disney movie?

8. Which movie sees the featured family win a holiday in a TV show titled 'A Pig in a Poke'?

9. What is the four-letter name of Mulan's alter ego when she is disguised as a male soldier?

10. What is the name of the President in 'My Fellow Americans'?

11. What is the name of the President in 'Airforce One'?

12. In 'Pulp Fiction' what is Yolande's nickname for her boyfriend Ringo?

13. In '9 to 5' what does Lily Tomlin's character accidentally add to her boss's coffee?

14. Which day of the week is common in the titles of three movies starring Ice Cube and John Witherspoon?

15. Which title character's surname is Rockatansky?

16. What is the first name of the pirate's daughter who becomes Juliet in 'Shakespeare in Love'?

17. Which 1997 movie was hyped: 'Nothing on Earth could come between them'?

18. Which 2011 chick-flic poster pictures five girls in pink and one in white?

19. Which movie added a romantic scene between Tom Cruise and Kelly McGillis when test audiences complained of no love interest?

20. Which movie's main role was taken by Tom Hanks after John Travolta turned it down?

1. Which liquid is officially recognised as a food in Bavaria?

2. What is Germany's most popular surname?

3. Which event did Germany become the first country in the world to clock-on to back in 1916?

4. Which annual event began as a celebration for the wedding of Prince Ludwig of Bavaria?

5. Which future fashion icon designed uniforms for the Hitler Youth and the Nazi Party?

6. Which is the world's tallest cathedral?

7. Which city boasts Europe's largest train station?

8. How many countries share a border with Germany?

9. What percentage of Americans claim at least partial German ancestry?

10. In which century did Germany invent the cuckoo clock?

11. Which nation knocked Germany out of the 2018 World Cup?

12. To the nearest million what is the population of Germany?

13. At what age does the average German woman give birth to her first child?

14. Which city boasts the world's largest zoo?

15. At which position does Germany lie on the list of Europe's biggest beer consumers?

16. Which German became a Barbie in 2009 to celebrate 50 years of the doll?

17. What term was first coined in 1866 by German biologist Ernst Haeckel?

18. What make the sounds 'Knisper! Knasper! Knusper! on German TV commercials?

19. Which German cathedral took 632 years to build?

20. What garden accessories were invented in Germany and later manufactured by the brother of U.K. prime minister John Major?

1. Which young farmyard animal is part of the inspiration for Italy's name?

2. Which famed chocolate magnate was Italy's richest man in 2018?

3. What were Romans protesting against when they handed out free spaghetti in 1986?

4. Which city is credited with popularising pizza?

5. Which 25-square-mile independent state is within Italy?

6. What killed an estimated 100,000 people in Sicily in 1693 that Italy suffers more regularly than any other European country?

7. Which ancient Roman building, in almost perfect condition, boasts the world's largest unreinforced concrete dome?

8. Which football term became 'meta' as part of Benito Mussolini's attempt to stamp out foreign words in Italy?

9. Who is known as Topolino in Italy?

10. What daily activity do Italians call 'passeggiata'?

11. What is Andrea Amati of Cremona credited with producing the first example of in the 16th century?

12. Which country is connected to Italy by the 22-mile-long Lotschberg Base Tunnel?

13. What are represented by the green, white and red stripes on the Italian flag?

14. In which decade did the Roman Catholic Church issue an apology for doubting Galileo's theory that the Earth orbited the Sun?

15. At what age do Italian citizens qualify to vote for members of the Senate?

16. In which century was the Leaning Tower of Pisa built?

17. Which race of people introduced pasta to Italy?

18. Which Italian tourist attraction raises three thousand euros in coins for charity in the average day?

19. How many times has Italy won the World Cup?

20. Which food will some Italian banks accept as collateral against loans?

1. Which is the only country to attract more tourists than Spain?
2. Which Spanish explorer was the first person to see Antarctica?
3. Which legendary Spanish hero is based on Rodrigo Diaz de Vivar?
4. Of which animal is the Spanish macaque Europe's only wild example?
5. What comes from the Meseta region of Spain that is often found in wine bottles?
6. Who knocked Spain out of the 2018 World Cup?
7. Which liquid does Spain account for 45% of the world's production of?
8. The world's oldest example of what can be found at El Castillo in northern Spain?
9. Which magnificent Moorish castle has a name that literally translates as 'The Red One'?
10. Which Spanish holiday island boasts the world's oldest and tallest Dragon Tree?
11. What is the British equivalent of a small mouse called Ratoncito Perez who visits Spanish children at night?
12. In 2008, who became the first Spaniard to win a Best Supporting Actress Oscar?
13. Which Picasso painting depicts an air strike during the Spanish Civil War?
14. What are thrown at the people of Bunol on the last Wednesday in August?
15. Which city's Puerto del Sol (Gate of the Sun) plaza is the physical centre of Spain?
16. What fruit do Spaniards traditionally eat twelve of as the clock strikes midnight on New Year's Eve?
17. What was voted 'the most meaningful book of all time' by 100 top authors in 2002?
18. Which Spanish city gained its own Guggenheim Museum in 1997?
19. Which major artist produced a tile mosaic that tourists walk on in Barcelona's famous Ramblas?
20. Which Spanish island gave birth to Mayonnaise and serves gin with breakfast?

. . . .

1. Which record was held by the Milau Viaduct when it opened in 2005?

2. Which literary name is given to at least one street in every town in France?

3. Which five-letter French word can mean 'hello' and 'goodbye'?

4. Which product, known to most children, takes its name from the French for 'oily chalk'?

5. Which fishy title was given to the heir to the French throne?

6. French men have Europe's lowest level of obesity but which Scandinavian country is the only one in Europe with a lower level of obesity than French women?

7. Who bragged he'd had a relationship with French First Lady Carla Bruni that she denied??

8. How many European countries have more ski resorts than France?

9. What was Mintel an early French version of?

10. Which Nobel Prize does France boast more winners of than any other country?

11. When the Bastille was stormed which financial crime were four of the seven prisoners in there for?

12. What statement is credited to Marie Antoinette but was actually coined ten years before she was born?

13. Which rock star's grave is the most-visited memorial in Paris's Pere Lachaise cemetery?

14. What was it illegal for women to wear in Paris following a law established in 1798 and not repealed until 2003?

15. Which is the oldest bridge across the Seine in Paris?

16. Which is the most-visited tourist attraction in Paris?

17. What colour is the cross indicating a French pharmacy?

18. What was 'Le Bon Marche' the world's first example of when it opened in Paris in 1838?

19. In which decade did France last dispatch a criminal on the guillotine?

20. Which French town is dubbed the Perfume Capital of the World?

. . . .

1. Which imperial dynasty lasted from 260BC to 1912AD?

2. How many countries cover a greater area than China?

3. What percentage of the world's population are Chinese living in China?

4. What do we take for granted that the Chinese invented in the 1300s and reserved for the use of their Emperors?

5. Which insects do Chinese children keep as pets that adults breed for fighting?

6. Into how many time zones is China divided?

7. What is China's most popular hobby?

8. What reason do foodie historians give for the Chinese use of chopsticks instead of knives and forks?

9. On September 27th, 2008, what did Zhai Zhigang become the first Chinese person to do?

10. What is the modern name for what had previously been called Yanking and Dadu?

11. In the Late Empire what did wealthy Chinese men and women grow to extreme lengths to signal their rank?

12. What did the Chinese start to use in the 14th century B.C. that Europeans didn't take up for another 2,300 years and the U.S. still hasn't adopted?

13. Which is the biggest dam in the world?

14. Which colour, symbolising happiness, is often worn by Chinese brides?

15. From the early 1930s, which was the only port in the world to accept Jews fleeing the holocaust without a visa?

16. Which fish is a Chinese symbol of strength?

17. What is signified by a Chinese woman starting to wear a single pigtail instead of her previous two?

18. Which is China's longest river?

19. What is the name of the world's largest public gathering space?

20. Which is China's most popular participation sport?

1. What does the Bay of Fundy have that are the highest in the world?

2. How many provinces are there in Canada?

3. Which is the world's second-largest French-speaking city after Paris?

4. Which is Canada's highest mountain?

5. Why is Canada's Wasaga Beach listed in record books?

6. How many Canadian islands are listed in the world's top ten largest?

7. What did Canada ban as being degrading to women in 1992?

8. What pet name do Canadians give to their one-dollar coin?

9. Which item of sports equipment, more closely associated with the U.S., was invented in 1883 in Canada?

10. What is the English meaning of Canada's motto: 'Mari Usque ad Mare'?

11. How many points has the maple leaf on the Canadian flag?

12. What was invented by Canadian's Chris Haney and Scott Abbot?

13. What became a province of Canada in 1949?

14. Which city brewed the first Molson beer?

15. Which is Canada's most popular cheese?

16. Which is the world's second-largest rodent?

17. What was the world's tallest, free-standing structure until 2007?

18. Which is Canada's smallest province?

19. How many Canadian cities have a population in excess of one million?

20. Into how many time zones is Canada divided?

. . . .

1. What have been allowed to rome freely through the corridors of St Petersburg's Hermitage museum following a decree of 1745?

2. What voluntary task do Russian citizens commonly undertake on the day known as Subbotnik?

3. Why are sections of Russian pavements cordoned off during winter?

4. Which parts of a chicken go into Russia's favourite kholodets soup?

5. Numerically, how does Russian etiquette require flowers be given to someone?

6. The word 'vodka' derives from the word 'voda', what does 'voda' mean?

7. Which British town witnessed nerve agent attacks in 2018 that were blamed on Russia?

8. Which emergency vehicle can rich Russian's hire to speed their way through Moscow traffic jams?

9. From what does Moscow take its name?

10. To which saint is the famous domed cathedral in Red Square dedicated?

11. Into how many time zones is Russia divided?

12. Which sport features in a DVD featuring Vladimir Putin?

13. Which is Europe's longest river?

14. Why is the town of Oymyakon Listed in record books?

15. Why did the Russian team arrive twelve days late for the 1908 Olympics in London?

16. What wasn't classed as an alcoholic drink in Russia until 2013?

17. Why does Russia's Lake Karachay find itself in record books?

18. Which food did Boris Yeltsin say he was looking for when discovered in his underwear, drunk, on Pennsylvania Avenue, Washington D.C. in 1995?

19. In exchange for drink products, what did Russia supply the Pepsi company with 17 of in 1990?

20. Why have polar bears taken to hanging around Russian airports?

. . . .

1. Why does $847.63 show on the supermarket cash register when Maggie is scanned in the opening credits of 'The Simpsons' back in 1989?

2. Who is Bart about to speak to when he places one of his regular calls to 764 84377?

3. Which word translates to 'Ouch' in Spanish editions of 'The Simpsons'?

4. What is Homer's favourite drink when 'The Simpsons' is shown in Arab countries?

5. Who is the only character in 'The Simpsons' with five fingers on each hand?

6. By what name is Jeff Albertson better known?

7. Which word from 'The Simpsons' was added to the Oxford English Dictionary in 2001?

8. Who co-wrote 'Do the Bartman' with Bryan Loren?

9. By what name is Robert Underdunk Terwilliger better known?

10. What Spanish exclamation was the first two words spoken by Bart Simpson?

11. Which wartime leader gave Millhouse Van Houten his middle name?

12. Who is the husband, and probably brother, of Springfield hillbilly Brandine Spuckler?

13. Who provides the voice of Sideshow Bob?

14. What is the connection between Bart Simpson and the numbers 36-24-26?

15. What is the movie-inspired name of the Springfield pastry shop?

16. Which 'Simpsons' duo have a pet iguana named Jub?

17. Who sings 'Maybe I'm Amazed' over the closing credits of 'Lisa the Vegetarian'?

18. What is Montgomery Burns' one-word catchphrase?

19. Who died in a freak accident involving a T-shirt cannon?

20. Who studied at the Calcutta Technical Institute before gaining his degree at the Springfield Heights Institute of Technology (S.H.I.T.)?

• •

Simply name the artist or act who had the biggest single or album hit with the song including a city in its title?

1. 'Nine Million Bicycles in Beijing'
2. 'Night Boat to Cairo'
3. 'Nice in Nice'
4. 'Alexa de Paris'
5. 'Born to Die in Berlin'
6. 'Hong Kong Garden'
7. 'Kingston Town'
8. 'Tokyo Joe'
9. 'Loco in Acapulco'
10. 'New Amsterdam'
11. 'Rotterdam (or Anywhere)'
12. 'Last Tango in Moscow'
13. 'Leningrad'
14. 'We're Going to Ibiza'
15. 'One Night in Bangkok'
16. 'Belfast'
17. 'London's Burning'
18. 'Kansas City Lights'
19. 'Leaving Las Vegas'
20. 'Memphis Tennessee'

• •

1. Which 1965 Bond movie was remade with the title 'Never Say Never Again'?

2. What is the most popular feature of Willie Wonka's 'Scrumdidilydumptious' chocolate bar?

3. Which of Disney's dwarfs has white, bushy eyebrows?

4. In 'When Harry Met Sally' which song from 'Oklahoma' does Billy Crystal sing with Meg Ryan?

5. In which language does Robin Williams sing 'My Way' in 'Happy Feet'?

6. What is the name of the computer waging war against humanity in 'Terminator 2: Judgement Day'?

7. Which deadly chemical does The Joker use in the 'Batman' movies?

8. Which movie's locations include the St Helen of the Blessed Shroud Orphanage?

9. What is the title character's seven-letter licence plate in 'Austin Powers: International Man of Mystery'?

10. For which European capital city is Trans Global Airlines Flight 2 heading when it leaves Chicago in the 1970 movie 'Airport'?

11. Which movie's title trio work as undercover dancers at the Treasure Chest nightclub?

12. In 'Wayne's World' which rock star do Wayne and Garth greet with the words: 'We're not worthy. We're not worthy'?

13. Which of the Three Musketeers has been played on screen by Oliver Reed, Keifer Sutherland and John Malkovich?

14. Which year saw the deaths of Charles Bronson, David Hemmings and Gregory Peck?

15. How many Oscars did 'Titanic' and 'The Lord of the Rings - Return of the King' each win?

16. Which movie ends with the words: 'I know a perfect place, you guys will love it. Trust me'?

17. Who is cloned in 'The Boys from Brazil'?

18. Whose version of 'Alfie' was tacked on to the movie soundtrack to qualify the song for an Oscar nomination?

19. For which movie did Marlon Brando report for work some 90 pounds overweight?

20. Which new invention does Butch Cassidy try out during the singing of 'Raindrops Keep Falling on My Head'?

1. What snack is John Cage's 'Ally McBeal' nickname?

2. Who had a hit (and 'hit' is a clue) with 'Theme From Miami Vice'?

3. What is the three-letter nickname of Rudy's pal Kenny on 'The Cosby Show'?

4. Who took his orders from Wilma Deering?

5. For what was Bobby Goldsboro's hit 'Hello Summertime' originally a commercial?

6. Who was the 'Monty Python' super hero?

7. Which state provides the setting for 'Knots Landing'?

8. Which TV cop series was a spin-off from the movie 'Prescription Murder'?

9. From what did the Lone Ranger make his mask?

10. Who replaced Arnold as boss at the 'Happy Days' cafe?

11. What was the world's most-watched TV programme until 'Live Aid' came along?

12. Which seasonal tree gave its name to the 'Red Dwarf' computer?

13. What is the philosophical name of Gomez's pet octopus in 'The Addams Family'?

14. Which shuttle, name checked in 'Bohemian Rhapsody', took crew back to the Starship Enterprise?

15. Why did Kojak suck that lolly?

16. Which TV show followed the exploits of Baker and Poncherello?

17. What colour is Mork's spacesuit?

18. What colour are Cliff's favourite socks on 'Cheers'?

19. How much does Louis charge his drivers for taking their phone messages on 'Taxi'?

20. Which animated TV dog gave his name to an island in Antarctica?

1. What is an akbash?

2. What shape is a freshwater angel fish?

3. Which bird was once so rare it became the symbol of the Royal Society for the Protection of Birds?

4. Which is the only country with native axolotls?

5. Which animal group includes the Aye Aye?

6. Which continent is the original home of the Bactrian camel?

7. What is a mouflon?

8. What is a bristle-head?

9. What is the four-letter name for the tail of a rabbit or hare?

10. What is the national animal of India?

11. Which animal has three species: Grevy's, Planes and Mountain?

12. Sperm whales are the largest creatures on Earth to posses what?

13. Which bird lays the smallest egg in relation to its size?

14. Which animal can be Javan, Sumatran, Indian, Black or White?

15. What colour is a polar bear's skin?

16. Which bird's feathers were prized for making early quill pens?

17. What is a female cat if a male is a tom?

18. Which is the only dog rated above the Bassett Hound for its sense of smell?

19. Which wild creatures does a Shiba Inus dog most look like?

20. What is the collective name for a group of pet cats?

1. What did 19 European nations agree to ban in January 1998?

2. Which was the first genetically modified salad ingredient available in British shops?

3. In which decade did Apple produce its first computer?

4. What did scientists announce they'd discovered in hairspray in 2008?

5. What is created by mixing alcohol with opium?

6. Which laboratory-grown organ was successfully transplanted into a rat for the first time in 2013?

7. What name did Harvard University give to the tiny, buzzing, flying robot they launched in 2013?

8. What did surgeons first wear in 1890?

9. What are measured on the Fujita Scale?

10. What did the Kyoto Protocol set out to limit?

11. In 2008, which became the fifth nation to land a probe on the Moon?

12. In which country is a carbon-neutral city named Masdar being built?

13. What title did tabloids attach to the H5N1 virus?

14. What is NASA's Kepler Observatory in orbit around?

15. Which international search engine that shares its name with a children's TV character was launched in 2009 by Microsoft?

16. What does the 'S' stand for in SIM Card?

17. What is the common term for aquaculture?

18. Which is the third prime number?

19. Which element has the atomic number 80 and the symbol Hg?

20. Which product's many varieties include fused silica and lead oxide?

1. Who was the seventh President of the U.S.A.?
2. Who directed the movie adaptation of the 'Lord of the Rings' trilogy?
3. Which singing member of the Jackson family's albums include 'The Velvet Rope' and 'Rhythm Nation'?
4. Which Jackson, known as the Queen of Gospel, sang at the 1963 March on Washington at the request of Martin Luther King Jr?
5. Which city is included in the names of Michael Jackson's only daughter?
6. Who was known as Jack the Dripper and died after drunkenly crashing his car into a tree?
7. In 2011, who was named the highest-grossing actor of all time with a fortune of $7.2 billion?
8. Who was the oldest member of the Jackson 5?
9. Who was lead guitarist with the Jackson 5?
10. Who caused controversy by claiming Dr Martin Luther King died in his arms and spoke his final words to him?
11. What was the nickname of Confederate leader Thomas Jonathan Jackson?
12. Who is dubbed the Queen of Rockabilly and is credited as the first woman to record a rock 'n' roll song?
13. Which future British Member of Parliament won Oscars for 'Women In Love' and 'A Touch of Class'?
14. Which member of the Jackson family's biggest-selling album was 'Heart Don't Lie'?
15. Which Jackson wrote the Eagles' hit 'Take It Easy'?
16. Which Jackson won the 110 metres hurdles World Championship title twice?
17. Which sci-fi series features a character called Daniel Jackson?
18. Which British comic writer featured Mike Jackson in his 'Psmith' novels?
19. Which Jackson is best remembered for his role as butler Hudson in 'Upstairs, Downstairs'?
20. By what first name was the mother of the Jackson 5 known?

1. What linked U.S. cops and the number 1,125 in 2015?

2. Which movie took $517 million on its opening 2015 weekend?

3. In 2015, which movie star gained worldwide publicity by spending $29 on a week's food as part of a Food Stamp challenge?

4. Which was the world's most widely distributed book in 2015?

5. What reason was given for 11.6 million people accessing the 'Vanity Fair' website to read about Caitlyn Jenner?

6. Where had 21 children been held, nine died and 107 were still incarcerated at the end of 2015?

7. Who did the U.S. beat 5-2 in the 2015 Women's World Cup final?

8. Which French satirical magazine was the target for terrorists in 2015?

9. What brought worldwide publicity to a band called Eagles of Death?

10. In which country was Baga which was wiped off the world map by Boko Haram in 2015?

11. Which budget airline lost a plane, passengers and crew when the depressed pilot crashed into the Alps in 2015?

12. In 2015, which country's first prime minister, Lee Kuan Yew, died at the age of 91?

13. Which capital city's Bardo Museum saw 22 visitors die at the hands of I.S. in 2015?

14. What three-letter name was given to the tropical storm that devastated Vanuatu in 2015?

15. In 2015, which U.S. city declared a state of emergency when police clashed with protestors at the funeral of a prisoner who died from spinal injuries?

16. In 2015, what became the first mainly Catholic country to vote in favour of and to accept gay marriage?

17. In 2015, with which country did the U.S. restore diplomatic ties after 54 years?

18. Which country celebrated 50-years of independence in 2015?

19. What is the name of the annual pilgrimage to Mecca that witnessed 2,200 deaths in a 2015 stampede?

20. What brought a boost to the value of shares in Chinese baby products in 2015?

1. After the U.S. and Canada which is the largest mainly English-speaking country in the Americas?

2. Which is the only Central American country without a Caribbean coast?

3. Which is the closest cathedral city to the Glastonbury Festival?

4. Which is the only language officially spoken in more than 50 countries?

5. Which Spanish city's sunshine record finds it dubbed the Frying Pan of Europe?

6. Which city is dubbed the Pearl of the Adriatic?

7. Which airport is known locally as Roissy?

8. Which European language has no word for 'please'?

9. What name did Bechuanaland adopt after independence?

10. If you collect your Mercedes Benz direct from the factory which city must you visit?

11. Which major tourist attraction takes its name from an Iroquois word meaning 'the strait'?

12. Which European city is at the centre of the world diamond trade?

13. Great Smoo is Scotland's largest example of which natural feature?

14. What is the Italian word for coast?

15. Which country attracts tourists to the Lion Gate of Mycenae?

16. Which tourist town hosted the 2005 weddings of Prince Charles and Elton John?

17. What is Chile's Ohos de Salado the world's largest example of above sea level?

18. What is Britain's most popular street name?

19. Which natural tourist attraction did Samuel Johnson describe as: 'Worth seeing but not worth going to see'?

20. Which is the world's largest peninsula?

1. Which famed British military man referred to his own troops as 'the scum of the Earth'?

2. What did Boris Yeltsin present to Bill Clinton during his 1994 visit to Russia?

3. What did Arawak Indians present to Christopher Columbus that he threw away because he didn't like the smell?

4. Who received a UNESCO award for establishing Iraq's public health system?

5. Which country lost the largest proportion of its population in World War II?

6. Which U.S. President walked to the altar with a three-month pregnant bride?

7. What did George W. Bush say he was giving up in 2003 out of respect for families of Americans killed in Iraq?

8. What did George W. Bush say was his common bond with Tony Blair?

9. Which President wears glasses on Mount Rushmore?

10. Who is credited with creating the term 'Rainbow Nation'?

11. Who was the first of Elizabeth II's offspring to obtain a divorce?

12. How did Ivan, Francis and Charley make headlines in 2004?

13. Who attracted an estimated 4 million audience on a 1995 visit to Manila?

14. For how many years did Prince Charles' marriage to Princess Diana officially survive?

15. What was KFC founder Harland Sander's highest military rank?

16. Which U.K. Prime Minister used the phrase: 'Fine words butter no parsnips'?

17. Which nation joined Britain in declaring war on Germany on September 3rd.1939?

18. What was closed to traffic for eight years following the Six Day War?

19. Which country received most of the funds raised by Live Aid?

20. How many astronauts died in the Challenger disaster?

1. Which month sees the first steins hoisted at Munich's annual beer festival?

2. What colour is a Remy Martin cognac bottle?

3. Which cocktail consists of vodka and orange juice with a float of Galliano?

4. Which drink is known as the Green Fairy?

5. What do Chinese people traditionally drink with their dim sum dumplings?

6. What do Russians traditionally drink with caviar?

7. Which drink was invented in 1898 by Caleb Bradham?

8. Which brand of whiskey comes from the world's oldest, still functioning distillery?

9. Which nationality was Captain Morgan, the pirate who gave his name to the popular rum brand?

10. Which English port claims to produce 'the world's smoothest gin'?

11. Which town on the Charente River refers to the evaporation from its casks as 'the angels' share'?

12. What promotes a Kir to a Kir Royale?

13. Which is the main spirit in a Margarita?

14. What is often added to a flaming Sambuca that ping across the surface of the drink?

15. Which fruit gives its flavour to Crème de Cassis?

16. Which French liqueur boasts of containing 27 herbs and spices?

17. In which month is Beaujolais Nouveau traditionally released?

18. What do Greeks call their resin-flavoured wine?

19. What is the most popular drink from the Douro Valley?

20. Of what is cenosillicaphobia a fear?

1. Which fashion house gained fame through its Bad Taste collection?

2. Which U.S. city boasted the world's first ATM specially designed for people wearing roller blades?

3. Which future fashion statement was first issued to the U.S. Navy in 1898?

4. Whose waif-like appearance in a 1993 advertising campaign for Calvin Klein drew criticism from Bill Clinton?

5. Whose 1995 appointment at Givenchy made him the first British designer to head a French haute couture house?

6. What do 29% of women cut from clothes, according to a Grazia magazine poll?

7. What are produced by Grendene under their Ipanema Gisele Bündchen label?

8. Which two-word term became accepted in 2005 to mean the jeans-related fashion crime of a visible roll of midriff fat?

9. Which city is home to the Dolce & Gabbana fashion empire?

10. Who brought funk to Chanel when he became their artistic director in 1983?

11. What is the name of the female component of the Italian Sixty fashion label?

12. Which sportswear company's logo consists of a large wave with a red mountain in the background?

13. Which future Grand Dame of fashion ran the Too Fast to Live, Too Young to Die memorabilia shop with Malcolm McLaren?

14. What was 19th century designer Charles Frederick Worth the first to add to his garments?

15. Which former Spice Girl was berated by the British Dental Association for wearing a fake lip ring during a performance?

16. Which country gave the world Ugg boots that became fleetingly fashionable in 2003?

17. Which 1960s fashion must-have has variously been credited to Mary Quant, John Bates and Courrèges?

18. What cheerleaders' flounced and layered garment became a short-lived 1980s fashion statement?

19. Which fashion house reportedly offered Princess Diana £1000,000 to appear on their catwalk, to celebrate her divorce from Prince Charles?

20. Who invented gabardine but is now better known as the name of a popular check design?

1. What is the main ingredient in a curry-cooling raita?

2. What is the name of Heston Blumenthal's restaurant in Bray, near Windsor, that has been hailed the best in the world?

3. Which world record was held by the Red Savina from 1994 to 2006?

4. Which bright yellow spice is hardest to wash out when you spill curry down the front of your shirt?

5. What is the Japanese word for raw fish?

6. Which animal provides the milk for traditional mozzarella pizza cheese?

7. Which little pet is called 'cuy' when served as food in South America?

8. Blond des Flandres is what tasty item?

9. In what is Duck Confit preserved?

10. What is the English translation of Rillettes, the popular French paté?

11. Which meat is in your Vietnamese hot dog if the menu says 'Thit cho'?

12. What has been minced to make your burger if the French menu lists 'haché de cheval'?

13. Which word on a menu indicates you are about to consume the first or second stomachs of a cow?

14. What do swiftlets contribute to Bird's Nest Soup?

15. Which organ from a goose or duck becomes Foie Gras?

16. What are matsuke an exotic and expensive variety of?

17. Which part of a chicken becomes 'Crete de coq' when used as a garnish on poultry dishes?

18. What colour is the extremely expensive Sterlet caviar?

19. Which milk pudding is made from the starch of a cassava plant?

20. Which herb do gourmets know as Chinese Parsley?

1. Which band named a track after basketball ace Magic Johnson?
2. Which song performed by Lady Gaga and Beyonce has a video continuing from where 'Paparazzi' left off?
3. Who went just by his last name on his 'Cherry Blue Skies' album?
4. Which king of disco co-wrote and appeared on the hit 'Get Lucky' with French duo Daft Punk?
5. Who was the first person with more than ten million followers on Facebook?
6. Which song on Whitney Houston's 'My Love Is Your Love' album has the same title as an early Elvis hit?
7. Which native New Yorker made a guest appearance on Gorillaz 2010 'Plastic Beach' album singing 'Some Kind of Nature'?
8. Who wrote 'All Along the Watchtower'?
9. Which band from Rockford captured their live sound on the album 'At Budokan'?
10. Who plays the deceased girl on Tom Petty's 'Mary Jane's Last Dance' video?
11. Who plays the incendiary guitar solo on Michael Jackson's 'Beat It'?
12. Which track introduced Roy Orbison to a whole new generation when it was heard in the movie 'Blue Velvet'?
13. Which band's 'Victory' tour boosted promoter Pepsi-Cola to a larger world market share than Coke for the first time ever?
14. Who sang the first solo line on U.S.A. For Africa's charity song 'We Are the World'?
15. Who released an album of Abba songs following her appearance in the movie 'Mama Mia: Here We Go Again'?
16. Which 1985 Cyndi Lauper hit had its original title in brackets when re-released as 'Hey Now' in 1994?
17. Which Madonna hit was condemned by the Vatican?
18. What advice does Paul Simon give to Gus in 'Fifty Ways to Leave Your Lover'?
19. Which famous family includes brothers George and Thomas whose deafness kept them out of the singing act?
20. Which movie provided the lyric for the White Stripes' hit 'The Union For Ever'?

1. Who is Captain von Trapp expecting to marry at the start of 'The Sound of Music'?

2. Which musical originated every amateur music society's favourite first song,. 'Another Op'nin, Another Show'?

3. Which musical is based on the play 'Green Grow the Lilacs'?

4. Which song from 'Paint Your Wagon' was covered by Michael Jackson?

5. Which clothing items has Henry Higgins lost at the end of 'My Fair Lady'?

6. Which city is the setting for 'The Threepenny Opera'?

7. At the start of 'Guys and Dolls' which sport are the guys talking about?

8. In which musical does one of the two lead characters claim to have 106 children with five more due next month?

9. Which song was almost dropped from 'Funny Girl' until Barbra Streisand announced she had already recorded it for single release?

10. Which is the biggest-selling song from 'A Little Night Music'?

11. Which song from 'Hair' was a worldwide hit for Oliver?

12. What was hyped 'The super soul musical'?

13. Which was the first British production to win the Tony Award for Best Musical?

14. Which stage musical begins with an announcement encouraging the audience to 'Let your cell phones and pagers ring willy-nilly'?

15. What are the first names of the two children in 'Mary Poppins'?

16. Which musical's characters include Jafar and Iago?

17. Which musical features the first ever Broadway score by Cyndi Lauper?

18. What is Millie's surname in 'Thoroughly Modern Millie'?

19. With whom does Berry Gordy have a bedroom scene in 'Motown the Musical'?

20. What reason did Barbra Streisand give for dropping out of the West End run of 'Funny Girl'?

• •

1. Which golf club's eighth hole is known as the Postage Stamp?

2. Which is the only position on a rugby field known by a number?

3. What did commercials once tell us Seve Ballesteros wouldn't leave home without?

4. Which name was common to six members of the Welsh rugby squad that played a 2004 Test against South Africa?

5. Which tennis star said in his autobiography: 'I was so wrecked on booze and pills that I asked my wife to shoot me'?

6. What is the alternative name for pétanque?

7. Which Spanish soccer squad play home games at the Bernabeu Stadium?

8. Which ball game is mentioned in Shakespeare's 'The Taming of the Shrew', 'Love's Labours Lost' and 'Richard III'?

9. Which sport's League teams include the Western Bulldogs and the Essendon Bombers?

10. Which game did Cherokee Indians refer to as 'the little brother of war'?

11. Who held the record for the most Wimbledon Men's Singles titles at the start of the 21st century?

12. By what four-letter title do the rules say bowls players should call their captain?

13. What starts a handball game if football starts with a kick-off?

14. Which country calls its Rugby Union minnows the Eagles?

15. Which tennis star's vocal outbursts resulted in her being dubbed the Queen of Scream?

16. With which club did David Beckham end his playing career?

17. Which game requires penthouses and a grille wall?

18. Which colour ball should be used in a rounders match?

19. Which three-letter term describes a tennis serve that has gone over the net after touching it?

20. How many minutes are there in each of the four periods of play in a water polo match?

1. Which city came second to London in the contest to host the 2012 Olympics?

2. Which 2004 Olympic event saw Brazil's Vanderlei de Lima attacked by a kilt-wearing former Irish priest?

3. In which sport was Irini Merleni the first woman to win gold when it was introduced to the Olympics in 2004?

4. Which country, banned from the Sydney Olympics for not allowing women into sport, had a female flag carrier in 2004?

5. Why did the Doves of Peace make news at the 1988 Seoul Olympics?

6. Which rock star from the far north sang at the 2004 Olympic opening ceremony?

7. Who said she would defend her Olympic tennis title in 2004 as it was the: 'Most treasured moment of my career'?

8. What did Athens say there would be 25% more of at their games than Sydney had at theirs?

9. In which city did the flame get stuck as it was supposed to rise to glory in 2000?

10. In what capacity did John Boland travel to the 1896 Olympics where he won a gold medal for tennis?

11. Who came second to the U.S.A. in the 2004 Olympic medal table?

12. Which is the final event of the Olympic Decathlon?

13. Who beat Riddick Bowe in the 1988 Seoul Olympics?

14. What must be at least 60 millimetres in diameter and three millimetres thick?

15. Which Olympic swimming event starts from inside the pool?

16. Which country in the Americas boycotted the the 1986 Los Angeles Games?

17. What advantage won France the gold medal in the 1900 Olympic croquet tournament?

18. Whose gold medal tally was second only to that of China at the 2004 Paralympics?

19. What got track champion Sureyya Ayhan banned from the 2004 Olympics when it was proved it wasn't hers?

20. Which is the longest Olympic running race to permit starting blocks?

1. On which day of the week did Ernest Hemingway refuse to travel?

2. Which Bare Naked Ladies album has lyrics by William Shakespeare?

3. Which Dickens novel follows the fortunes of an orphan named Pip?

4. Who died in 2014 after creating poet-detective Adam Dalgliesh?

5. Who wrote the book that became the musical 'Chitty Chitty Bang Bang'?

6. What snack was a book title for Ben Elton and a hit record for Hot Butter?

7. Which British playwright won the 2005 Nobel Literature Prize?

8. What did Samuel Johnson say the talk will be about when two Englishmen first meet?

9. Which Wilkie Collins novel introduced Godfrey Abelwhite?

10. Which author's final words were reportedly; 'Go away, I'm alright'?

11. In which Daphne Du Maurier novel is Mrs Danvers the housekeeper at Manderley?

12. Which Stanley Kubrick movie is based on an Arthur Schnitzier novella?

13. Which music icon controversially won the 2016 Nobel Prize for Literature?

14. Which Shakespeare character says; 'But soft, what light through yonder window break

15. Which Ray Bradbury novel begins; 'It was a pleasure to burn'?

16. What three words complete P.G. Wodehouse's quip; 'I hadn't the heart to touch breakfast. I told Jeeves to ...'?

17. What is Barbara Vine's nom de plume?

18. What did Robert Burns refer to as 'Great chieftain o' the pudding race'?

19. Which word completes Jonathan Swift's quote; 'He was a bold man who first ate an ...'?

20. Which Belgian creator of a very famous detective claimed to have slept with 10,000 women?

1. Who is the first baby born and the first person killed in the Bible?

2. Who gave his name to fantasists and has five heroic dreams ending with him facing a firing squad?

3. How many men are on the Dead Man's Chest in 'Treasure Island'?

4. Which band perform the concert attended by the killer in the novel 'American Psycho'?

5. Which food does Ben Gunn dream of while on 'Treasure Island'?

6. Which decade of her life has Bridget Jones entered when she starts writing her diary?

7. By what other name is Aragorn known in 'Lord of the Rings'?

8. What ate the parents of James in 'James and the Giant Peach'?

9. In which city did Miss Jean Brodie do most of her teaching?

10. Which 'Watership Down' rabbit shares his name with a nut?

11. What creature is Benjamin in Orwell's 'Animal Farm'?

12. Which vegetable is mentioned only four times in the Complete Works of Shakespeare but 21 times in 'Dracula'?

13. Which four-letter word describing the coming together of two people was first recorded in 'Romeo and Juliet'?

14. In 'The Hitch Hiker's Guide to the Galaxy' what number is the answer to 'Life, the Universe and Everything'?

15. How many members of the Fellowship of the Ring are Hobbits?

16. Which pub is Frodo in when he first slips on The Ring?

17. In which novel do prostitutes play out a fantasy that they are the Prophet Mohammed?

18. What is the fruity name of Hercule Poirot's secretary?

19. Which superhero is pictured on detective Elvis Cole's coffee mug?

20. How old is Jane Eyre at the start of Charlotte Bronte's novel?

. . . .

1. Which first name is common to Toulouse Lautrec and Matisse?
2. Which Munch painting was stolen during the 1994 Winter Olympics and again during the 2004 Games?
3. Who painted 'Madonna of the Yardwinder' which was stolen in 2003?
4. For whom did Vincent van Gogh intend the piece of his ear he cut off and eventually gave to a prostitute?
5. Which city's main gallery displays Botticelli's 'The Birth of Venus'?
6. Which brand of English beer lines up alongside the champagne in Manet's painting 'The Bar at the Follies-Bergere?
7. Which city boasts the world's largest permanent collect of Van Gogh's paintings?
8. Which city's Picasso Museum boasts a vast collection of early works donated by the artist in 1970?
9. Who is the subject of the painting by Louis le Brocquy unveiled to celebrate the reopening of the Irish National Portrait Collection in 2003?
10. Whose 'Las Medians' is a star of the Prada collection in Madrid?
11. Which museum advertises its most famous painting as being Rembrandt's 'The Night Watch'?
12. Which politician's portraits filled an entire room at the 1989 Andy Warhol touring exhibition?
13. Whose wife, Gala, was buried intact in 1982 even though he'd previously announced he intended eating her?
14. What nationality was Goya?
15. Whose exquisite works include 'Girl With a Pearl Earring'?
16. What colour dress is the woman wearing in Jan van Eyck's famed 'Arnolfini Portrait'?
17. Which artist's works sometimes reference his homosexuality, as in 'We Two Boys Together Clinging'?
18. Who based his paintings such as 'Whaam!' on frames from comic books?
19. Which famous painting is spoofed on a McEwans Beer label?
20. Which artist married Italian porn star and politician Ilona (Ciccionlina) Staller?

1. Which sport is the subject of 'The Endless Summer'?

2. Which movie's main, male role did Gary Cooper reject, warning: 'It will be the biggest flop in Hollywood history'?

3. Which 2012 movie tells the story of tourists caught in the 2004 Indian Ocean tsunami?

4. In which 2002 movie does New York's iconic Flatiron Building become the offices of the Daily Bugle?

5. Who is pictured with Tom Cruise on posters for 'Eyes Wide Shut'?

6. Which 1993 box office hit was set on Isla Nublar near Costa Rica?

7. What is the title of the movie if marching marines sing the 'Mickey Mouse Club' theme song?

8. Who is Borat obsessed with in his 2006 mockumentary?

9. What is the four-letter name of Alicia Silverstone's 'Clueless' character?

10. Which movie was hyped: 'Makes 'Ben Hur' look like an epic'?

11. Who won his first Oscar in 2001 with the song 'Things Have Changed' from the movie 'Wonder Boys'?

12. From what does Roy make his first model of Devil's Tower in 'Close Encounters of the Third Kind'?

13. What has the American Film Institute named the Best Movie Song of All Time?

14. What is made from the fat removed at the liposuction clinic in 'Fight Club'?

15. What disability is suffered by Tobey Maguire's jockey character in 'Seabiscuit'?

16. At the start of 2018, what was the highest-grossing animated movie of all time?

17. What does Shrek create from his earwax?

18. Who played the Manchurian Candidate before Denzel Washington reprised the role?

19. Which movie duo reside at 66 West Wallaby Street?

20. Which 2006 remake of a 1933 classic brought director Peter Jackson a $20 million preproduction pay packet?

. . . .

1. Which TV show's characters use a fast food restaurant named the Chum Bucket?

2. Which brand of cigarettes are smoked by Marge Simpson's twin sisters?

3. Which wanted man did 'South Park' refer to as 'Farty Pants'?

4. Which TV duo were dubbed PJ and Drunken after a 2018 drink-drive incident?

5. What did Dutch 'Big Brother' contestant Tanja Savanna have during a show that boosted ratings considerably?

6. What is the name of the fictional fashion house in 'Ugly Betty'?

7. Which TV show features paper manufacturers Wernham-Hogg?

8. What is the name of Kirstie Alley's bar manager character on 'Cheers'?

9. Robin Williams was Mork but who was Mindy?

10. What is the name of Bo and Luke Duke's sister?

11. Which show featured D&D Advertising and Shooter's Bar?

12. Which service does Nick Riviera provide for the citizens of Springfield?

13. Who shot J.R. in 1980?

14. Which TV sleuth lives at Cabot Cove?

15. Which former U.S. President took an acting role in 'Dynasty'?

16. What is the name of the family who gave Gordon Schumway, their visitor from the planet Melmac, the name ALF?

17. What was Elvis on 'Miami Vice'?

18. Who was leader of the Decepticons?

19. Who died 475 years before Mark Rylance played him on 'Wolf Hall'?

20. Which TV series launched 1993's best-selling toy range for boys?

. . . .

1. Which gas causes the bends when released from a diver's blood?

2. From which part of a willow tree was aspirin originally extracted?

3. In 1953, which was the first human internal organ to be successfully transplanted?

4. Which Asian capital city boasts a parasite museum where you can marvel at a 9-metre tapeworm removed from a man?

5. What is the common name for the disease rubella?

6. Which complaint takes its name from Medieval Italian words for 'bad air'?

7. Where is your tragus?

8. How many pairs of ribs has the average human?

9. What is stored in the gall bladder?

10. What is the common name for the fluid expelled from the human body by the process of lacrimation?

11. Where in your body will you find your aqueous humour?

12. A sprain is an injury to which tissue?

13. What is surrounded by amniotic fluid?

14. How many vertebrae are there in the lumber spine?

15. Where are ganglion cysts most commonly found?

16. What does a transient ischemic attack often precede?

17. Jaundice is a sign of disease in which organ?

18. Which fibrous tissue connects muscle to bone?

19. An evisceration is an injury to which area of the body?

20. Which stage of labour ends when the cervix is fully dilated?

. . . .

1. Which is the only breed of cat without retractable claws?

2. Which Aussie animal has no nipples so feeds its young with milk that oozes from its body?

3. Which Aussie animal can be Common, Northern Hairy-Nosed or Southern Hairy-Nosed?

4. Apart from body size, what is the most obvious physical difference between African and Indian elephants?

5. Which milk, found in most supermarkets, comes from a ruminant?

6. How many finger-like projections has an African Elephant at the end of its trunk?

7. How many neck vertebrae has a giraffe compared with a human's seven?

8. Which animal has the highest blood pressure?

9. Which is the fastest-running bird found wild in Britain?

10. What were solar panels planned for Antwerp Zoo in 1997 intended to supply for elephants?

11. What was the first animal to be beheaded and dissected in space?

12. What form the greater part of a polar bear's diet?

13. What are bontebok, blesbok and bongo all types of?

14. How many tusks has an Indian rhinoceros?

15. Which animal requires a 3.5 metre appendix to deal with its diet of gum leaves?

16. Which island boasts 40 different species of lemur?

17. What did a 2012 research project discover had the strongest bite-force of any terrestrial animal that ever lived?

18. Which language turned 'earth pig' into 'aardvark'?

19. In 2015, what were there reported to be 3,000 of in the wild compared with 5,000 captive in the U.S.?

20. Which is the world's slowest animal?

• •

1. What do you collect if your treasured items include a Waterman 42 and a Parker Dufold?
2. What did Clive Sinclair launch in 1985 with a price of £399?
3. Which car was 'tested by dummies, driven by the intelligent'?
4. What were most commonly forgotten and left in rooms by hotel guests in 2017?
5. Which city boasts the headquarters of Alpha Romeo?
6. What did 84% of people in Britain own at the start of 2005 but only 54% of Americans and 42% of Canadians?
7. From what does Bluetooth take its name?
8. In which year did Apple launch its first iPod?
9. What does BSA stand for on a motorcycle badge?
10. What was revolutionary about the shape of the iPod second generation when it was launched in 2006?
11. Which country's Perodua Kelisa has been described as 'the worst car in the world'?
12. What are the small glass dispensers called that spirit bottles are upturned over in most bars?
13. What were the two colours of the first Swiss Army Knife?
14. Which was the world's largest airliner in 2007?
15. Which smartphone's models include the Porsche and the Curve?
16. Which was the first company to install airbags as standard equipment in all its cars?
17. Which music format, at its peak in the 1970s, lasted until the 1990s at radio stations where it was used for playing jingles and commercials?
18. What did Frank Nasworthy transform in 1973 by adding polyurethane wheels?
19. Which was the tallest structure in the world before New York's Chrysler Building overtook it in 1930?
20. For what purpose was a sleeve supplied with the 1990s Motorola 8800X cell phone?

1. Which British singer did fashion guru Karl Lagerfeld describe as 'The new Brigitte Bardot'?

2. What was Alicia Silverstone voted the world's sexiest example of in a 2004 poll?

3. Who was voted the world's most over-exposed celeb in 2005?

4. Which rock star joked of claims he enjoyed six-hour tantric sex sessions that this included; 'dinner, a movie and maybe a lot of begging'?

5. Who dated Gene Simmons and Ryan O'Neal between marriages to her business manager Robert Silberstein and Norwegian tycoon Arne Naess Jr?

6. Which rock star sued his band's former stylist to get his hat and pants back?

7. Where did Melanie Griffith say a man needs to touch a woman to drive her crazy?

8. Whose marriage to country crooner Kenny Chesney lasted all of four months?

9. Which rock star was the subject of biographies by both of his wives in 2005?

10. Which Welshman did Libby Purves describe as 'The rudest man I ever met, and unattractive, pock-marked as an Easter Island statue'?

11. What did actor Larry Hagman claim never to do on Sundays?

12. In 2008, which supermodel became the subject of the largest gold statue made since ancient Egyptian times?

13. By what name did Prince Charles call Camilla while he was still married to Diana?

14. What were Elizabeth Taylor and future husband Larry Fortenski both attending when they first met?

15. What was Italian Reinhold Messner the first person to reach alone?

16. What nationality was Marco Polo, who called China, Cathay?

17. Which city is the Dalai Lama's spiritual home?

18. Which pop diva tangled tongues with Madonna and Christina Aguilera at the 2003 MTV Awards?

19. Who ended up paying $177,000 in legal fees after suing an amateur snapper for taking photos of her Malibu estate?

20. What is the relationship between Johnny Depp and Betty Sue whose name is tattooed on his left bicep?

1. What did 81 students wear while riding a roller coaster to set a world record in 2004?

2. Which appropriate date is National Condom Day in the U.S.?

3. Who has a brother called Bells Nichols in France?

4. Who is the most recent U.S. President to undergo surgery for haemorrhoids whilst in office?

5. What caused damage to the heat-shield tiles resulting in the delay of a 1995 Space Shuttle launch?

6. What do many Japanese enjoy as a Christmas dish having confused the company's founder with Santa Claus?

7. Which fruit do U.S. Marine Corps soldiers superstitiously refuse to allow in their tanks?

8. What do members of the First Presleytarian Church of Elvis the Divine do six times each day in memory of the King?

9. What must you register as before taking part in a duel in Paraguay?

10. Which European country's national anthem pledges loyalty to the King of Spain?

11. In a 2006 poll what did the majority of British men say was the first thing they desired after waking up in the morning?

12. What did a 2014 survey reveal are missing from 57% of home-cooked meals in the U.S.?

13. Which U.S. state has towns called Bumpass, Nuttsville and Ben Hur?

14. What does a misomaniac hate?

15. What's the link between Theodore Roosevelt and Jonathan Edwards?

16. In 2003, what did Morocco offer Iraq 2,000 of as a means to detonate mines?

17. Which is the most regularly shop-lifted product in British supermarkets?

18. In 2001 what did the U.N. declare to be a basic human right?

19. Why doesn't America display the Pilgrim Fathers' ship Mayflower in a museum?

20. Which country produced the first easy-stacking, cube-shaped watermelon?

. . . .

1. Who became Soviet leader after the death of Leonid Brezhnev?

2. Who became the first member of the royal family to be banned from driving?

3. Why did the main character in 'Tootsie' dress like a woman?

4. In a popular TV commercial, what was a photographer eating that caused him to miss a shot of roller skating pandas?

5. What flavour were Pint Pot Chews?

6. What shape were Yobbo sweets?

7. Which South Coast resort gained a temporary tourist attraction when the Greek freighter Athena grounded on its beach?

8. Which northern football club took eight years to get back into the top division after being relegated in 1982?

9. Which 1980s sweets came with stickers featuring such characters as Dead Ted, Nervy Nigel and Boney Joanie?

10. Which very popular TV show's main characters were James, Tristan and Siegfried?

11. What delayed the 1987 Cheltenham Gold Cup by almost one and a half hours?

12. What did Home Secretary Douglas Hurd ban from all British broadcasts?

13. Which archaeologist and Israeli military leader always appeared in public wearing a black eye patch?

14. Who died in 1988 and was referred to by Bono as 'The finest singer on the planet'?

15. Which newspaper cartoon strip was adapted for TV with James Bolam in the title role?

16. Who was the star of 'The Antiques Roadshow' until his death in 1985?

17. In 1987, whose super middleweight win made him the first man to take world boxing titles in five different weights?

18. What were British rent payers first permitted to buy in October 1980?

19. What did 50% of British women have in 1981, the highest percentage in the European Community?

20. Which island was the setting for 'Bergerac'?

• •

1. How old was Lady Diana Spencer when she became engaged to 32-year-old Prince Charles?

2. What nickname was given to early morning keep-fit guru Diana Moran?

3. How many times did Cambridge win the Boat Race in the 1980s?

4. What colour was the shirt worn by the very brave guy who stopped the tanks in Tiananmen Square?

5. Who was labelled 'Interesting' by 'Spitting Image'?

6. Which hyphenated two-word phrase describing extreme surprise was first used in the 1980s?

7. Which overweight dance troupe appeared regularly on TV with Les Dawson?

8. What were Turkish peasants selling for £2,000 each to make news in the 1980s?

9. What did Margaret Thatcher say was 'never intended to cater for all the needs in life'?

10. Which member of the Beach Boys died in the same year as Karen Carpenter?

11. Which Barry Ryan oldie gave punk rockers The Damned their only top-ten hit?

12. Who was given a four-year sentence for violating Soviet air space after landing in Red Square?

13. Which Irish town suffered an IRA attack at its 1987 Remembrance Day parade?

14. What was taught at Maplin's Holiday Camp by Yellow Coats Barry and Yvonne?

15. Who became the first Brit to win the U.S. Masters?

16. Which TV show discouraged 'two in a bed' and regularly showed losers what they could have won?

17. Who became a Monster Raving Loony politician after being cleared of running a brothel in the 'Sex on the Stairs' case?

18. Which ice cream was stolen by a passing gondolier?

19. Which character replaced Grandad on 'Only Fools and Horses'?

20. What was the adult version of 'TISWAS'?

1. Which early morning radio presenter coined the phrase 'White Van Man'?
2. What was the nickname of eco-warrior Daniel Hooper?
3. Which MM was hyped by the Sun as the girl for the Thrillennium?
4. Who were the first all-female act to sell one million copies of an album in the U.K. yet only managed one chart-topping single?
5. How many children moved into Downing Street with Tony and Cherie Blair?
6. Which former BBC reporter took one of Britain's safest Tory seats from Neil Hamilton?
7. Who covered her feet with black socks but didn't take her gloves off when she visited a temple in Pakistan?
8. Which Disney movie was slammed as 'commercial plundering' by the family of Victor Hugo?
9. Where was the Union Flag replaced with ethnic designs?
10. Which football star was depicted as Christ in a controversial painting titled 'The Art of the Game'?
11. Which sport did the British Government urge the E.U. to exclude from a ban on tobacco sponsorship?
12. What resulted in the 1997 Scottish World Cup qualifier against Belarus being delayed from Saturday to Sunday?
13. In 1996, who became the youngest Wimbledon women's singles winner of the 20th century?
14. Which planet was battered by comet Shoemaker-Levy 9?
15. Which city was the home of serial killers Fred and Rosemary West?
16. Which sport banned silicone head implants, used to bring competitors to the minimum height of 68 inches?
17. Which author and relative of Princess Diana claimed she'd given John Major his 'Back to Basics' slogan?
18. Which Westminster councillor and Tesco heiress orchestrated a multi-million vote-rigging scandal?
19. What did Eva Herzigova advertise with the slogan 'Hello Boys'?
20. What was Rod Stewart's former wife, Alana, the first Hollywood celebrity to sue a surgeon over?

• •

1. What title was won by Mandy Smith in 1994 and Tracy Shaw in 1996?

2. Which Yorkshire brass band's Carnegie Hall concert posters were condemned by Americans as being racist and sexist?

3. What new name was given to girlie group Touch that included Michelle Stephenson in its original line-up?

4. What did Mr Cohen and Mr Greenfield introduce to Britain in 1994?

5. What reason did Tory M.P. David Ashby give for sharing a bed with a male colleague?

6. Why did gas and electricity suddenly become more expensive on 1st April 1994?

7. Which was Oasis's first U.K. number-one single?

8. Which word completes the rugby poster slogan: 'It's not the winning - It's the taking ...'?

9. Which British romcom won five 1995 BAFTAs in direct competition with 'Forrest Gump'?

10. Who quit the Rolling Stones in 1993?

11. What did you play with if Fifi had an apartment in France and Midge owned a flower shop?

12. What were British doctors allowed to do in 1990 for the first time in 130 years?

13. What were Soviet citizens allowed to own in 1990 for the first time since the 1920s?

14. In what form did Ian Paisley sell for £462 at a London auction?

15. What continued in England and Wales after being banned in Scotland in 1991 as 'extortion and theft'?

16. Where was Florence Nightingale replaced by Charles Dickens?

17. Which Teenage Mutant Ninja Turtle didn't originally share his name with an artist?

18. What was the somewhat unfortunate title of the last song at the Freddie Mercury tribute concert?

19. What cost £1.60 at Wimbledon in 1990 that went up to £1.70 in 1993?

20. What is the Japanese word for 'Empty orchestra'?

• •

1. How many bars are there on the cell window of a Monopoly board.

2. Which chess piece is known as 'Fou' in France and 'Laufer' in Germany?

3. Which Aussie pop star made news by beating Salman Rushdie at Scrabble?

4. How many points has the star on a Chinese Checkers board?

5. Which is the highest number on the Game of Life spinning wheel?

6. How many different types of square are on a Pictionary board?

7. How many letters fit across a standard Scrabble board?

8. How do players bring a new piece to the track in a game of Ludo?

9. Which board game's tiles include two mountains, a gold mine and a dragon?

10. Which game do patients first play in the bathroom in 'One Flew Over the Cuckoo's Nest?

11. Which country introduced Trivial Pursuit to the world?

12. Which game is the subject of Murray Head's hit record 'One Night in Bangkok'?

13. Which word is printed on the square where all players' tokens should start a game of Monopoly?

14. Who takes the place of Colonel Mustard in The Simpsons Cluedo?

15. How many playing pieces does each player use in a game of Chinese Checkers?

16. How many blank tiles are supplied with a game of Scrabble?

17. How many question categories are to be found in a standard game of Trivial Pursuit?

18. What colour is the car on the Monopoly board FREE PARKING space?

19. How many rows of squares separate the two sets of pawns at the start of a game of chess?

20. What do players of the travel game GO have to collect in the countries they visit?

. . . .

1. Which word means cooking under a source of heat in the U.K. but is cooking above a source of heat in the U.S.?

2. Into which dressing is a Waldorf Salad tossed?

3. What does consommé become when served with floating globs of savoury custard?

4. What is the English name for chou rouge?

5. Which English county did Daniel DeFoe credit with producing probably the best butter but the worst cheese?

6. Which creature's liver appears on menus as tomalley?

7. What is the name for green Japanese horseradish?

8. How has fish been cured if it is described as ceviche?

9. What has wine become if it is described as pricked?

10. What turns cheese on toast into a buck rarebit?

11. What name do Americans give to a frying pan?

12. Which meat is essential to garbure soup?

13. Which alcoholic drink gives its flavour to traditional Cumberland Butter?

14. What turns mayonnaise into aioli?

15. Which liqueur boasts of being made to Bonnie Prince Charlie's own secret recipe?

16. Which part of a pig's anatomy can be served as a Bath Chap?

17. What is the main ingredient in a Glamorgan Sausage?

18. What was voted the most popular restaurant and takeaway dish in the U.K. at the start of the 21st century?

19. Which country produces the 1970s top-selling wine, Mateus Rosé?

20. What is the maximum number of Michelin stars a restaurant can hold?

1. What do two racks of lamb become when their bones are interlinked to be served with the fat facing outwards?

2. What is the visible 'kick' in a wine bottle?

3. Which domino appears on the Dominos Pizza logo?

4. What is the British name for what the French call fromage de tete, or cheese of the head?

5. Which member of the onion family is essential in Vichyssoise Soup?

6. Which amphibian shares its name with a hot grill often found above the oven in a professional kitchen?

7. What are you likely to find on a dining table that Peugeot were manufacturing before they started building cars?

8. Which island produces Talisker whisky?

9. What do Greeks insist becomes more tender if you beat it 99 times on a rock?

10. Who always referred to his legion of fans as 'Gastronauts'?

11. What name is usually given to chivda when served as a spicy snack in British pubs?

12. What is the sour part of a Whiskey Sour?

13. Which fruit is used to dress Sole Veronique?

14. Which pub snack is technically known as arachis hypogaea with a sprinkling of sodium chloride?

15. Which Dutch lager has the date 1615 on its cans?

16. Which pastry is used to make éclairs and profiteroles?

17. What is the main ingredient in laver bread?

18. Which common four-letter word can mean an osculation or a cocktail containing cream?

19. Which sauce should enrobe Eggs Benedict?

20. What has one if it's Danish, two if it's British and three if it's Club?

1. Which Scottish rock diva performed 'Into the West' in 'The Lord of the Rings - The Return of the King'?

2. Which alternative name for someone on a horse is also the list of dressing room requirements in a rock band's contract?

3. Which century is it at the start of the movie 'Wall-E'?

4. What is the name of the dotty old military man who was a resident at Fawlty Towers Hotel?

5. Which TV series included an episode titled 'Owl Stretching Time'?

6. Which band's music features in the flop, stage retelling of the movie 'Desperately Seeking Susan'?

7. How many suspects are brought together for the line-up in 'The Usual Suspects'?

8. Which band sang about 'pushing an elephant up the stairs'?

9. What was Duran Duran's Bond song?

10. What were Guns n' Roses told they couldn't do on stage that resulted in them cancelling a concert in 2006?

11. In 'Fargo' what does the guy sell who hires the inept henchman to kidnap his wife?

12. In which movie does someone tell Bill Murray: 'Everyone is going to Gobbler's Knob'?

13. Which band denied that their 'Hail to the Thief' album was a comment on the 2000 U.S. election?

14. What was intended to prevent breeding in 'Jurassic Park'?

15. Which Shakespeare play includes the quote: 'Though this be madness, yet there is method in it'?

16. Who did David Bowie say would be 'astounded and amazed if he realised to many people he is not a sex symbol but a mother image'?

17. Which of the Three Tenors has a name meaning 'Peaceful Sunday'?

18. Which internationally renowned circus was formed in Canada in 1984?

19. Which letter does Eminem reverse in his name?

20. What are Dame Edna Everage's favourite flowers?

1. Which country attracts tourists to its Leptis Magna ancient Roman site?

2. Which city's attractions include the Spanish Steps?

3. What is the unit of currency in the British Virgin Islands?

4. Which Caribbean island is divided into the three counties of Cornwall, Middlesex and Surrey?

5. Which floor number is dropped in many Chinese hotels because it sounds like 'death' in Mandarin Chinese?

6. Which country's World Heritage sites include the Head Smashed-In Buffalo Jump?

7. Which sweet treat do guests traditionally each receive five of at an Italian wedding?

8. Whose castle towers over Disneyland Paris?

9. Which city's tourist attractions include a cemetery that is the home of approximately a million living people?

10. Which town takes tourists to the shack where Elvis was born?

11. Where will you find the largest Greek population in any city outside Greece?

12. Which group of islands were the Beach Boys visiting when they sailed around Nassau on the Sloop John B?

13. Which is the largest city in the Caribbean?

14. Which U.K. city's airport is situated at Lulsgate Bottom?

15. Which Florida location calls itself the Diving Capital of the World?

16. Which Greek island boasts the underwater temple the turtle swims past in 'For Your Eyes Only'?

17. Which animal gives its name to the island in the middle of Niagara Falls?

18. What are natives of Lesbos called?

19. Which is the closest city to the sandbar of the Lido that gave its name to public bathing pools?

20. Which of New York City's international airports is not in New York State?

1. Which battle, remembered by Americans, saw the deaths of Ulstermen Robert Evans, Samuel Burns and James McGee?

2. Which insect was Napoleon's symbol for industry and efficiency?

3. Which is the only surname shared by a British Prime Minister and an American President?

4. Which European nation finally got around to giving its women a vote in 1971?

5. What delayed Prince Charles' and Camilla's wedding by a day?

6. Who was described by one of his guards as: 'Obsessed by cleanliness and a lover of Doritos'?

7. In 2005, who topped a BBC poll to find the politician with the least pleasant voice?

8. What has been banned in the British House of Commons since 1693?

9. In which capital city was Yasir Arafat at the time of his death?

10. Which daughter of an Albanian grocer won the first Pope John XXIII Peace Prize?

11. Why did many Jehova's Witnesses fail to book summer vacations in 1976?

12. Whose excuse for not meeting Soviet leaders was: 'They keep dying on me'?

13. To which country was Julius Caesar referring when he said: "Veni, Vidi, Vici' (I came, I saw, I conquered')?

14. What were introduced to British motorists in 1983 but not to Venetian gondoliers until 2005?

15. Which job did the guys claim to be doing when they raised the Argentine flag over the Falklands to start the 1982 war?

16. What did the U.S. Senate finally get around to apologising for in 2009?

17. Who was assassinated in October 1984 whilst walking to an interview with actor Peter Ustinov?

18. What name was given to the beret-wearing vigilantes from New York who spent time patrolling the London Underground?

19. What title was given to Winnie Mandela's gang of murdering thugs?

20. Which was Britain's last African colony?

1. What are Sienna X and Fake Bake?
2. Which Italian company launched its still-popular bamboo-handled handbag in 1947?
3. Who was the only model listed as earning more than Kate Moss at the start of 2007?
4. Who designed clothes for Shakira's 'Oral Fixation' tour and was the first to announce he wanted to employ Kate Moss after her drug scandal?
5. Which company launched Stella McCartney's jacket, hyped as 'suitable for sport vegetarians'?
6. Which 1980s fashion statement was popularised by the 'Dynasty' TV show?
7. Which movie is credited with turning ripped sweatshirts revealing one naked shoulder into a fashion statement?
8. Which staple garment for ballet practice became a 1980s fashion essential?
9. What did 'Sex and the City's' Carrie claim no woman in Manhattan would ever be seen wearing in her hair in public?
10. What is the name of Lionel Richie's adopted daughter who became a model for Bongo Jeans and a 'face' of Jimmy Choo?
11. What is the four-letter name of J Lo's first perfume?
12. Who wore nothing but a necktie on the January 2009 cover of GQ magazine?
13. Who showed off her figure in a Guy Laroche gown when collecting her 2005 Oscar?
14. Which item of dance gear made it to the High Street in 2006 in pink glitter and leopard-skin print?
15. Which underwear brand sold for a reported $70 million in 2007?
16. Who became the 'face' of Gucci in 2007?
17. What type of product was Chanel's limited edition Black Satin?
18. How many petals has the iconic Mary Quant flower logo?
19. Who introduced his Peasant Look in 1976?
20. Which stone became a fashion essential when Lady Di sported one at the heart of her engagement ring?

1. What is the surname of the one member of ZZ Top who doesn't have a beard?

2. Which hit tells the story of a woman who claims Michael Jackson is the father of her child?

3. Which single was credited to Wham! in the U.S. but to George Michael in the U.K.?

4. What costume did David Bowie don for his 'Ashes to Ashes' video?

5. On which night of the week does Abba's 'Dancing Queen' strut her stuff?

6. Which band backed Prince immediately prior to the New Power Generation?

7. Who killed himself in a state of depression unaware he was reportedly about to be offered the gap left by Roy Orbison in the Travelling Wilbury's?

8. What is the one-word title of Coldplay's first album?

9. What is the actual title of what is known by most Fab Four fans as the 'White Album'?

10. At what age did Amy Winehouse, Kurt Cobain, Jim Morrison, Brian Jones, Janis Joplin and Jimi Hendrix all die?

11. With which band was Rod Stewart vocalist immediately prior to going solo?

12. Which band featured Jeff Lynne and Roy Wood after they moved on from the Move?

13. What is the title and year of release of the Van Halen album that includes their classic 'Jump'?

14. Who is pictured clutching a rifle on the cover of Iron Maiden's 'Women in Uniform'?

15. Who had the world's biggest hit with 'Momma Told Me Not to Come', a song written by Randy Newman for Eric Burdon?

16. Which supergroup featured Eric Clapton, Ginger Baker, Ric Grech and Steve Winwood?

17. Which Boston-based rockers once bailed out 53 concert attendees arrested for smoking dope?

18. Which Chuck Berry classic was sent into space with Voyager 1?

19. What are the only things the woman is wearing on the cover of Robert Plant's 'Pressure Drop'?

20. Which band temporarily morphed into the Village Green Preservation Society?

1. Who composed 'Also Sprach Zarathustra' which features in '2001: A Space Odyssey'?

2. Which Beethoven symphony features predominantly in 'A Clockwork Orange'?

3. Which 1979 Ridley Scott movie features excerpts from Mozart's 'Eine Kleine Nachtmusik'?

4. Which city is the setting for Puccini's 'Madame Butterfly'?

5. In which city did Chopin tinkle as a tot?

6. Which country is the setting for 'Aida'?

7. Who composed the music for Austria's national anthem?

8. Which country is the setting for Mozart's 'Magic Flute'?

9. Who composed 'Piano Sonata No. 14 in C Sharp Major', commonly known as the 'Moonlight Sonata'?

10. Which of Handel's oratorios includes the 'Hallelujah Chorus'?

11. Which Wagner opera includes the tune everyone knows as 'Here Comes the Bride'?

12. Of whom did Joseph Haydn say; 'Posterity will not see such talent as his again for 100 years'?

13. Whose music did Mark Twain describe as; 'Not so bad as it sounds'?

14. Whose 'Unfinished Symphony' is the theme for Gargamel, the villain in 'The Smurfs'?

15. Why are thirteen notes from Francisco Tarrega's 'Gran Vals' guitar masterpiece amongst the world's most recognised pieces of music?

16. Who wrote 'The Young Person's Guide to the Orchestra'?

17. Which opera by Mozart is seen as the sequel to Rossini's 'The Barber of Seville' despite being written some thirty years earlier?

18. During which appropriate year did Gustav Holst compose 'Mars - The Bringer of War'?

19. Which Austrian composer's body is buried with two skulls?

20. What is the popular title for Dvorak's 'Symphony No. 9 in E minor'?

1. Which nation's rugby squad is nicknamed the Cherry Blossoms?

2. What colour should the centre spot be in ice hockey?

3. What name is given to the point in a marathon where a runner experiences sudden, dramatic fatigue?

4. What name appeared on posters advertising heavyweight Yorkshire wrestler Shirley Crabtree?

5. Which athletic world records have only been recognised since 1987?

6. What do the rules of athletics say must 'not be objectionable, even when wet'?

7. Who was the world's highest-paid sportsperson at the start of the 21st century?

8. What name is given to the area within which the baton must change hands in a relay race?

9. Who was the first boxer to defeat Muhammad Ali?

10. Who traditionally helps the winner of the U.S. Masters golf tournament into his prize green jacket?

11. What is the scoring target in a game of korfball?

12. Which country attracts skiers to Kitzbuhel?

13. What takes its name from a Greek term meaning 'exercise naked'?

14. Over how many weeks is the Tour de France contested?

15. What is Alaska's official state sport?

16. What name is given to the activity in which humans roll around in giant hamster balls?

17. Which world championship, staged in Nepal, was won by Scotland in 2004 and 2005?

18. Which football team, known as the Terriers, was promoted to the Premiership in 2017?

19. What breaks the fall when tombstoning?

20. On which racecourse do horses encounter Tattenham Corner?

. . . .

1. Which country won the most medals at the 2018 Winter Olympics?

2. Which city's 1972 Olympics made an international star of Olga Korbut?

3. Which South West English town was the base for 2012 Olympic sailing events?

4. What first took place at the 1968 100m final that has become commonplace since?

5. What does a home country athlete traditionally hold in the left hand while taking the Olympic oath?

6. Which men's Olympic event can include the crucifix?

7. How many throwing events are included in the Olympic decathlon?

8. Which local sport-related items were removed from the streets of Barcelona during the 1992 Olympics?

9. Who carried the British flag at the start of the 2016 Olympics?

10. In which sport did Jade Jones win a gold medal for Britain at the 2016 Olympics?

11. Which city tried to round up and inoculate an estimated 44,000 stray dogs in time for the 2004 Olympics?

12. Which was the favourite condom flavour with athletes at the 2000 Olympics?

13. How many lanes has an Olympic swimming pool?

14. Why didn't Ben Johnson compete in the 1980 Olympics even though he was selected for his country's team?

15. What four letters were emblazoned on a Soviet Olympic vest prior to 1992?

16. Which city blamed Michael Jackson's 'They Don't Talk About Us' slum-shot movie for losing their bid to host the 2004 Olympics?

17. What was Marie Porvaznikova of Czechoslovakia the first athlete to do during the Olympics?

18. Which country retains the Olympic rugby title having won it when last contested in 1924?

19. Which sport brought Britain's only gold medal in the 2002 Winter Olympics?

20. Which Olympic city is served by Kimpo International Airport?

1. What is Inspector Morse's first name?

2. Which English habit did sleuth Dr Gideon Fell claim to be working on?

3. Which sleuth did G.K. Chesterton base on a parish priest he met in Bradford?

4. Which month on the calendar is represented by the girl who goes to law school in 'Legally Blonde'?

5. Which Graham Greene classic tells the story of Pinkie Brown?

6. What is the name of Jamie Fraser's time-travelling wife in Diana Gabaldon's 'Outlander' series?

7. What type of animal is Ratty in 'Wind in the Willows'?

8. Which animal gets sour grapes in one of Aesop's fables?

9. What is the name of the ape who adopts Tarzan?

10. Who is the third musketeer along with Athos and Aramis?

11. What is the surname of Emma in Jane Austen's novel?

12. What is the Great Gatsby's first name?

13. What is the name of the young chimney sweep in Charles Kingsley's novel 'The Water Babies'?

14. For what has Tom Joad served a prison sentence at the start of the 'Grapes of Wrath'?

15. What is the name of John le Carrés' 'Perfect Spy'?

16. What is the surname of the kids taken to Neverland by Peter Pan?

17. Who is the hero of Terry Pratchett's 'Night Watch'?

18. Who visits Narnia with Peter, Susan and Lucy in 'The Lion, the Witch and the Wardrobe'?

19. Which novel features Jean Valjean who is known by his former prison number 24601?

20. Who is the hero of Raymond Benson's novel 'The Facts of Death'?

1. What's the maximum number of rupees tourists are allowed to take into India?

2. Which fruit is India the world's largest exporter of, with Brazil in second place?

3. What are you about to visit if your entrance ticket comes with a bottle of water and a pair of white shoe covers?

4. What is thrown around during the annual festival of Holi?

5. Which game is derived from the Indian pastime 'chaturanga'?

6. Which spicy colour on the Indian flag represents courage and sacrifice?

7. Which unusual aspect of the statues at the temples of Khajuraho makes them a major tourist attraction?

8. What was first used for practical purposes in India and known as 'morning dew' to Roman emperors who wore it?

9. What name was given to the practice whereby Indian widows threw themselves onto their husband's funeral pyre?

10. What is Sanskrit for 'snow abode'?

11. What will an Indian grasp to signify repentance or sincerity?

12. Which location in Rajasthan is known as the Pink City?

13. Which year saw the end of British rule in India?

14. Which religion is followed by approximately 80% of Indians?

15. What was the former name of Mumbai, home of the Indian film industry?

16. Which title, meaning 'Great Soul', was adopted by Mohandas K. Gandhi?

17. Which is India's national fruit?

18. Which is the world's largest civilian employer with some 16 million workers?

19. Into how many time zones is India divided?

20. How many seasons does India recognise each year?

. . . .

1. Which meat is traditionally in Kabuli Pulao, the national dish of Afghanistan?

2. Which semolina-based salad is the national dish of Algeria?

3. What is the national dish of Belgium?

4. Which is the other main ingredient along with kidney beans in Costa Rica's national dish Gallo Pinto?

5. Which country serves Ropa Vieja, shredded steak in tomato sauce with a side of plantain fritters and rice?

6. Which European country's frikadeller is like a flattened meat ball?

7. What name does Equatorial Guinea give to its national dish of corn, beans, peppers and tomato?

8. Which large shell contains the ingredient for one of the Bahamas' favourite dishes?

9. Which sauce tops a Greek moussaka?

10. Which is the main spice in Hungarian goulash?

11. What is the main ingredient in an Indian sambar?

12. What traditionally tops an Indonesian nasi goreng?

13. Which meat makes an Irish Stew?

14. What is the nori element in Japanese sushi?

15. In which liquid is the rice soaked for Malaysian nasi lemak?

16. Which meat goes into a traditional Moroccan tagine?

17. Which is the only meat product acceptable in a Dutch stamppot?

18. Which country claims the Pavlova as a national dish?

19. Which vegetable predominates in Polish bigos?

20. What is the name of traditional Swiss potato patties?

The
Quizmaster's
QUIZ BOOK

• •

Name the song containing each lyrical line. All the songs were released by the Beatles as singles (a-sides or b-sides) in the U.K.

1. 'I think I got it off the writer, sittin' down by the rhythm review'.

2. 'And while I'm away, I'll write home every day'.

3. 'Let me whisper in your ear, say the words you long to hear'.

4. 'This could only happen to me. Can't you see, can't you see'

5. 'All the lonely people. Where do they all come from?'

6. 'You keep all your money in a big brown bag in a zoo'.

7. 'You say 'go, go, go''.

8. 'But if you want money for people with minds that hate, all I can tell you is brother you have to wait'.

9. 'Where did we lose the touch that seemed to mean so much?'

10. 'And when the broken-hearted people living in the world agree'.

11. 'He got muddy water, he one mojo filter'.

12. 'Saving up your money for a rainy day, giving all your clothes to charity'.

13. 'When the sun shines down, and sip their lemonade'.

14. 'One way ticket yeah, it took me so long to find out'.

15. 'I'm so glad that she's my little girl, she's so glad she's telling all the world'.

16. 'And though we may be blind, love is here to stay and that's enough'.

17. 'Just cast an eye in her direction'.

18. 'Man buys a ring, woman throws it away. Same old thing happens every day'.

19. 'And the band begins to play'.

20. 'Who finds the money when you pay the rent'.

Name the song containing each lyrical line. All of the songs were released by the Rolling Stones as the a-side of singles in the U.K.

1. 'I was drowned, I was washed up and left for dead'.
2. 'The dogs begin to bark, hounds begin to howl'.
3. 'She gets her kicks in Stepney, not in Knightsbridge anymore'.
4. 'I'm sorry girl but I can't say, feeling like I do today'.
5. 'She spent all my money, playing her high-class games'.
6. 'My love bigger than a Cadillac'.
7. 'Who's all dressed up like the Union Jack and says I've won five pounds'.
8. 'If I look hard enough into the setting sun. My love will laugh with me before the morning comes'.
9. 'Go catch your dreams before they slip away'.
10. 'Remember I'll always be around and I know, I know like I told you so many times before'.
11. 'Your servant am I and will humbly remain'.
12. 'And a man comes on and tells me how white my shirts can be'.
13. 'Have you seen her dressed in blue? See the sky in front of you'.
14. 'Doing things I used to do, they think are new'.
15. 'Made damn sure that Pilate washed his hands and sealed his fate'.
16. 'I bet your momma was a tent show queen and all her boyfriends were sweet sixteen'.
17. 'You know I've got a woman and she lives in the poor part of town'.
18. 'The lamps are lit the moon is gone I think I've crossed the Rubicon'.
19. 'I watched you suffer a dull aching pain, now you've decided to show me the same'.
20. 'Through the light your face I see, baby take a chance, baby won't you dance with me'.

Name the song performed by the artist from the lyric clip provided.

1. Irene Cara: 'Take your passion and make it happen'.
2. Britney Spears: 'The reason I breathe is you, boy you got me blinded'.
3. Beyonce: 'When I talk to my friends so quietly, who he think he is'.
4. Mary J. Blige: 'Better know your friends or else you'll get burned'.
5. Jewel: 'Lay me out in firelight let my skin feel the night'.
6. Kylie Minogue: 'Threw away my clothes, got myself a better wardrobe'.
7. Katy Perry: 'Do you know that there's still a chance for you 'cause there's a spark in you?'
8. Laura Branigan: 'Will you marry me for the money, take a lover in the afternoon?'
9. Mariah Carey: 'You know sugar never ever was so sweet'.
10. Leona Lewis: 'I need a place where you can run, if you need a shoulder to cry on'.
11. Nina Simone: 'Got my neck, got my boobs, got my heart, got my soul'.
12. Amy Winehouse: 'There's nothing you can teach me that I can't learn from Mr Hathaway'.
13. Tina Turner: 'It may seem to you that I'm acting confused'.
14. Aretha Franklin: 'I didn't know what was wrong with me 'till your kiss helped me name it'.
15. Janis Joplin: 'You're out on the street looking good and baby deep down in your heart I guess you know it ain't right'.
16. Joni Mitchell: 'And I dreamed I saw the bombers riding shotgun in the sky'.
17. Patti Smith: 'Vengeful aspects become suspect and bending low as if to hear'.
18. Bonnie Raitt: "If I could buy your love I'd truly try my friend'.
19. Annie Lennox: 'Some of them want to abuse you, some of them want to be abused'.
20. Gladys Knight: 'Bought a one-way ticket to the life he once knew, oh yes he did, he said he would'.

ONE HUNDRED & THIRTY-TWO
NATIONAL SPORTS

• •

A list of countries - name their official national sport which is spelt out with every other letter missing.

1. Afghanistan — -u-k-s-i
2. Argentina — -a-o
3. Anguilla — -a-h- r-c-n-
4. Bangladesh — -a-a-d-
5. Bermuda — -r-c-e-
6. Bhutan — -r-h-r-
7. Canada (Summer) — -a-r-s-e
8. Canada (Winter) — -c- h-c-e-
9. Chile — -h-l-a- r-d-o
10. China — -a-l- t-n-i-
11. Dominican Republic — -a-e-a-l
12. Georgia — -u-b- u-i-n
13. Japan — -u-o w-e-t-i-g
14. Lithuania — -a-k-t-a-l
15. Madagascar — -u-b- u-i-n
16. Norway — -r-s- c-u-t-y -k-i-g
17. South Korea — -a-k-o-d-
18. Slovenia — -l-i-e s-i-n-
19. Pakistan — -i-l- h-c-e-
20. Sri Lanka — -o-l-y-a-l

1. For which movie did Humphrey Bogart win his only Best Actor Oscar?

2. Who collected the 1954 Best Actor Oscar for 'On The Waterfront'?

3. Which movie brought Leonardo DiCaprio his 2016 Best Actor Oscar?

4. Which role won the 2014 Best Actor Oscar for Eddie Redmayne?

5. Who was the first Frenchman to win the Best Actor Oscar?

6. Who won a Best Actor Oscar for 'The King's Speech'?

7. Who became the youngest Best Actor Oscar-winner for 'The Pianist'?

8. Which movie brought Denzel Washington his 2001 Best Actor Oscar?

9. Who collected the 1995 Best Actor Oscar for 'Leaving Las Vegas'?

10. Who won consecutive Best Actor Oscars in 1993 and 1994?

11. Which movie brought Al Pacino his only Best Actor Oscar?

12. Who was the first person to win the Best Actor Oscar three times?

13. Which was Robert De Niro's only Best Actor Oscar-winning role out of five nominations?

14. How many Best Actor Oscars has Dustin Hoffman won out of seven nominations?

15. Which movie brought Sean Penn his 2008 Best Actor Oscar?

16. What was Forest Whitaker's winning role in 2006's 'The Last King of Scotland'?

17. Playing which great soul star brought Jamie Foxx the 2004 Best Actor Oscar?

18. What's the name of Kevin Spacey's character in 'American Beauty'?

19. What's the name of Michael Douglas' character in 'Wall Street'?

20. Which movie brought Jack Nicholson the 1997 Best Actor Oscar?

1. Who was nominated for Best Actress six times, winning for 'Gaslight' and 'Anastasia'?

2. Which movie brought Audrey Hepburn her only Best Actress Oscar?

3. Who won Best Actress for 'Klute' and 'Coming Home'?

4. To the start of 2018, how many Best Actress Oscars had Meryl Streep won out of her 15 nominations?

5. Who, at the age of 80, became the oldest Best Actress Oscar-winner?

6. Which movie brought Jessica Lange her 1994 Best Actress Oscar?

7. Who was the first black winner of a Best Actress Oscar?

8. What was Reese Witherspoon's winning role in 'Walk the Line'?

9. In 2007, who became the first person to win the Best Actress Oscar for a French-language movie?

10. Who became the youngest Best Actress Oscar-winner for her role in 'Children of a Lesser God'?

11. What is the surname of Alice in 'Still Alice' the title role that brought the Best Actress Oscar to Julianne Moore?

12. Who played Jeanette (Jasmine) Francis to win the Best Actress Oscar for the movie 'Blue Jasmine'?

13. Who won the 2009 Best Actress Oscar in competition against Helen Mirren, Carey Mulligan, Gabourey Sidbe and Meryl Streep?

14. Who won the 2009 Best Actress Oscar for playing Virginia Woolf in 'The Hours'?

15. Which movie saw Hilary Swank's Best Actress Oscar performance as Brandon Teena?

16. Which movie brought about Gwyneth Paltrow's notoriously tearful acceptance speech?

17. Who played Annie Wilkes in 'Misery'?

18. Which movie brought Jodie Foster her first Best Actress Oscar?

19. Which movie brought Julie Andrews her only Best Actress Oscar?

20. Which movie brought Vivien Leigh her second Best Actress Oscar after 'Gone With The Wind'?

Note: Rock and Roll Hall of Fame is abbreviated to R&R HoF in all questions.

1. Which city is the home of the R&R HoF?
2. Over which Great Lake does a wing of the R&R HoF jut out?
3. Which wife of a rock star cut the ribbon to officially open the R&R HoF?
4. Who are the only band to equal the Beatles' eight entries in the R&R HoF's 'Songs That Shaped Rock and Roll'?
5. Which city has hosted the most R&R HoF induction ceremonies?
6. Why did the Crickets and the Comets have to wait until 2012 to be inducted into the R&R HoF?
7. Who were the first duo to be inducted into the R&R HoF?
8. How many years after their first commercial record release is an act eligible for the R&R HoF?
9. Which Welsh singer accused the R&R HoF of gender bias when she delivered the 2013 John Peel Lecture?
10. Which British band played a tribute to the recently deceased Chuck Berry when they were inducted to the R&R HoF in 2017?
11. Which R&R HoF inductee wrote 'Ain't No Sunshine' while working as an aircraft toilet manufacturer?
12. Who was the last Beatle inducted into the R&R HoF as a solo performer?
13. Who backed Bob Dylan when he went electric but were not inducted into the R&R HoF until 2006?
14. What is the minimum percentage of the committee's votes a nominee must achieve to be inducted into the R&R HoF?
15. Who were Frankie Lymon's backing band?
16. Which female group were inducted into the R&R HoF alongside the Beatles, Beach Boys, Drifters and Bob Dylan?
17. As a member of which band did Jeff Beck enter the R&R HoF in addition to his solo induction?
18. Which solo guitarist was inducted in 1994 on his eighth nomination?
19. Which singer of 'Cry to Me' was nominated a record ten times prior to his induction in 2001?
20. Which British female was inducted in 1999 alongside Paul McCartney?

• •

Simply name the famous person who originally said or sang each of the following.

1. 'Everyone has the right to pronounce foreign names as he chooses'.

2. 'A woman becomes an extension of a man's ego, like his horse or his car'.

3. 'A woman must have money and a room of her own if she is to write fiction'.

4. 'If I chance to talk a little wild, forgive me. I had it from my father'.

5. 'Bugger Bognor'.

6. 'Abroad is unutterably bloody and foreigners are fiends'.

7. 'The only way to get rid of temptation is to yield to it'.

8. 'Ice formed on the butler's upper slopes'.

9. 'He was born an Englishman and remained one for years'.

10. 'Pam I adore you, Pam you great big mountainous sports girl'.

11. 'We are a grandmother'.

12. 'Money doesn't talk, it swears'.

13. 'I want to be the white man's brother, not his brother-in-law'.

14. 'Those in the cheaper seats clap. The rest of you rattle your jewellery'.

15. 'The ballot is stronger than the bullet'.

16. 'In starting and waging war it is not right that matters, but victory'.

17. 'I love Paris in the springtime'.

18. 'People talking without speaking, people listening without hearing'.

19. 'Turn on, tune in, drop out'.

20. 'Television is an invention that permits you to be entertained in your living room by people who you wouldn't have in your home'.

1. What begins: 'The hottest day of the summer so far was drawing to a close …'?

2. Who says 'Goodbye' to Alice in Wonderland then falls off a wall?

3. Which literary animal is the hero of 'Splash Mountain' rides at Disney theme parks?

4. Who is Huckleberry Finn's best friend?

5. What title is given to the stage version of 'Wind in the Willows'?

6. What is the name of the boy who has the adventure with Raymond Brigg's 'Snowman' in the TV movie?

7. From whose vegetable patch does Peter Rabbit steal?

8. What animal is Curious George?

9. What is the name of the boy who is the wildest thing in 'Where the Wild Things Are'?

10. What has 'terrible tusks and terrible claws and terrible teeth and terrible jaws'?

11. Which night of the year is it at the start of 'The Polar Express'?

12. Which birthday did 'The Cat in the Hat' celebrate in 2014?

13. Which story's early version saw the evil Queen drop down dead after being forced to dance wearing red-hot iron shoes?

14. What does Mary Lennox discover in Yorkshire that is a very famous book title?

15. What is the name of the girl who is carried off by the Big Friendly Giant?

16. What is the title of the book that brought fame to the Psammead who has to grant one wish every day?

17. Whose door is topped by a sign reading 'Mr Sanders'?

18. What nationality was the original Pippi Longstocking?

19. What is Anne of Green Gable's surname?

20. Which Roald Dahl book includes a cat called Lipshen?

1. Who or what is 'Descending a Staircase' in the title of one of Marcel Duchamp's most famous paintings?

2. Who is the subject of Pauline Boty's 'The Only Blonde in the World'?

3. Which painter is the subject of the movie 'A Bigger Splash'?

4. Which lane did Hogarth depict to demonstrate the bad side of booze?

5. Which natural product was an essential element of Chris Ofilli's 1998 Turner Prize winner?

6. Which animal is George Stubbs recognised as one of the greatest ever painters of?

7. Who had relationships with Damien Hirst, Gary Hume and Angus Fairhurst and pictured herself sitting on a lavatory?

8. By what title is Gainsborough's painting of young Jonathan Buttal internationally known?

9. Which Brotherhood was founded in 1848 by John Everett Millais, Dante Gabriel Rossetti and William Holman Hunt?

10. Whose best known works include 'Monarch of the Glen'?

11. Which great British artist's embarrassingly erotic drawings were found in 2005 even though John Ruskin claimed to have burnt them?

12. Which very famous sailor's boyhood is captured in one of the most recognisable paintings by John Everett Millais?

13. Who went through a phase of faxing his works to exhibitions?

14. What colour is the headband worn by Vermeer's 'Girl With a Pearl Earring'?

15. Which Prime Minister's wife destroyed a portrait of her amateur artist husband by the brilliant Graham Sutherland?

16. In which decade was surrealism at its height?

17. Which German artist had a bird alter-ego called Lolop?

18. Which dotty painting technique is most famously employed by Seurat and Pissarro?

19. Whose gold-encrusted portrait of Adele Bloch-Bauer sold for a reported $90 million in 2006?

20. Whose two paintings of 'La Danse' are recognised as key points in the development of modern art?

1. Which award-winning movie was described as a 'Gay cowboy romp'?

2. Which movie's lovers are played by Tom Hanks and Antonio Banderas?

3. Which movie gave birth to the term 'Bunny Boiler'?

4. Which duo were on 'A mission from God'?

5. Which movie coined the phrase; 'Lunch is for wimps'?

6. Who plays Foxxy Cleopatra in 'Austin Powers in Goldmember'?

7. To which prison is Andy Dufresne sent after being convicted of murdering his wife and her lover?

8. Which musical romcom collected six Oscars in 2017?

9. With which animals is Gibbs found sleeping in 'Pirates of the Caribbean - Curse of the Black Pearl'?

10. Which movie introduced the character Lucas Jackson?

11. Which 2002 movie with a distance as its title features the Notorious B.I.G. track 'Juicy'?

12. In which Asian city does Bill Murray tweet Scarlett Johannson in 'Lost in Translation'?

13. Which movie hears the line; 'As far back as I can remember I always wanted to be a gangster'?

14. Who pulled out of filming 'Panic Room' after being injured filming 'Moulin Rouge'?

15. What is Citizen Kane's dying word?

16. Which city's name is first seen outside the hospital in 'Silence of the Lambs'?

17. Which three-letter name is given to the little girl who causes chaos in 'Monsters, Inc.'?

18. Which three words complete the phrase from 'Crimson Tide'; 'We're here to preserve democracy ...'?

19. Which 1999 teen sex comedy features Fat Boy Slim's track 'The Rockafella Skank'?

20. Which sport does Murphy first ask to watch at the group session in 'One Flew Over the Cuckoo's Nest'?

. . . .

1. Who were banned from TV in Afghanistan in 1992?

2. Which city was said to be suffering from 'Scarlett Fever' when 400 hopefuls lined up to audition for a TV remake of 'Gone With the Wind'?

3. Which British actress played Nanny G in a 'Cheers' cameo role?

4. Which TV series introduced an Ethiopian character tastefully named Starvin' Marvin?

5. Whose song 'Woke Up This Morning' was the theme for 'The Sopranos'?

6. How old is Bart Simpson?

7. How many times did Buffy the Vampire Slayer die during the TV series?

8. Which was the first TV show to have its title printed on the face of a credit card?

9. What is Norville Rogers' nickname on the 'Scooby Doo Show'?

10. To whom did Mork report at the end of each day on Earth?

11. What did Homer Simpson describe as: 'Teacher, mother, secret lover'?

12. Which was the most financially successful animated TV series prior to 'The Simpsons'?

13. What is the name of SpongeBob SquarePants' pet snail?

14. According to the sign outside Springfield Nuclear Plant, how many days since the last accident?

15. Which breed of dog was Fang, Lieutenant Columbo's pet?

16. Which 'Friends' character was the brother of Rachel's high school friend Monica?

17. Which state provides the setting for 'Family Guy'?

18. Which TV series was hyped: 'Every parent's nightmare'?

19. What does Lester Nygaard sell in 'Fargo'?

20. What is the name of the teen who becomes Teen Wolf?

• •

1. Which vitamin is mostly required for blood coagulation?

2. What can be skeletal, smooth or cardiac?

3. Which vitamin was isolated from fish liver oil in 1917?

4. What is the common name for clavicle?

5. At which point do the humerus, radius and ulna all meet?

6. Encephalitis is inflammation of which organ?

7. What is the alternative name for nares?

8. Which word describes a persistent, intense, irrational fear of a specific object, situation or activity?

9. Behind what will you find your T10 spinal nerve root?

10. How many branches has the human trachea?

11. Which term describes a fracture where one side of the bone is broken and the other only bent?

12. What is the common way of saying metacarpals on patellae?

13. What is the alternative name for capacitance vessels?

14. What are of different sizes if a paramedic diagnoses anisocoria?

15. In which joint could you suffer a Colles Fracture?

16. Which common term best describes a gravid person?

17. In 2009, what fashion fad did the British Dental Association warn can cause death?

18. In 2002, what did California scientists claim can be measured to indicate a person's sexual orientation?

19. What can someone suffering from abasia no longer do?

20. What are extra hairy if a man is described as dasypygal?

1. Into which street does Ernie gallop?

2. What does Ernie wear upon his chest?

3. What is the name of the widow who Ernie loves?

4. What is the address of the widow who Ernie loves?

5. Which three words did people use to describe Ernie's favourite widow?

6. What did Ernie get from his favourite widow three times every week?

7. What did Ernie's widow friend want to do?

8. Which milk did Ernie think was best?

9. What was Ernie's reaction when his widow friend said she'd be happy if the milk went up to her chest?

10. Who was Ernie's rival and where was he from?

11. With which tarts did Ernie's rival tempt the widow?

12. What did Ernie's rival have that were such a size they nearly turned the widow's head?

13. What almost caused the widow to swoon?

14. What did Ernie's rival offer the widow every morning?

15. What did Ernie's rival offer the widow every night?

16. What time was it when Ernie kicked his rival's horse?

17. What did Ernie have in his hand when he rushed into the street to challenge his rival?

18. Which flavour yoghurt knocked the bun from the hand of Ernie's rival?

19. What hit Ernie underneath his heart?

20. What caught Ernie in the eye?

1. Which fruit's name is based on a word meaning testicle from the Nahutati language of Mexico?

2. What colour are the flowers of a coffee bush?

3. What is the attractively named shito the smallest example of?

4. What did Ronald Reagan once claim cause 80% of air pollution?

5. Which seasonally saucy fruit is sorted for ripeness by bouncing?

6. Which plant provides linseed oil?

7. Which is the national tree of France, Germany and Poland?

8. What is the Stinking Bishop that gave its name to a Dorset cheese?

9. Which alternative name is usually given to pot marjoram on a pizza menu?

10. Which scented garden blossom is used to flavour tea in China?

11. Which product's popularity has resulted in the destruction of much of Indonesia and Malaysia's rainforests?

12. Which fruit comes from the citrus paradisi tree?

13. Which seasonal plant does the U.S. state of Connecticut list as its most important tree crop?

14. What is the coco de mer palm tree's claim to a place in record books?

15. What is the difference between a herb and a spice?

16. Which beer ingredient is from the same plant family as marijuana?

17. What is the fruity, more popular, name for the Purple Grenadilla?

18. In 1973, what destroyed the world's most isolated tree?

19. If you carve your loved one's initials on the trunk of an oak tree how many inches higher will it get each ten years?

20. What finds the titan arums a place in record books?

• •

1. What was first patented in Britain in 1750 with a recipe mostly of fish and fish bones?

2. Which seasonal item did Addis first create in the 1930s employing the same machine they used to produce toilet brushes?

3. What did electric kettles lack for the first eight years of their existence?

4. What did Robert Yeates invent in 1855 that people had previously used a hammer and chisel for?

5. What was English statesman and philosopher Francis Bacon trying to develop when he caught the cold that killed him?

6. What did Thomas Angrove develop in 1965 that he hoped would make the corkscrew redundant?

7. What will you find in most bathrooms that was invented in 1892 by Dr Washington Sheffield?

8. Which country started heating homes with crematorium generated energy in 1997?

9. What is the best known brand-name for borosilicate glass?

10. What did a 2002 British Journal of Plastic Surgeons claim puts 40% of young men at risk of injury because they don't know how to unfasten it properly?

11. What are the most dangerous things Turkish troops are credited with inventing at the Battle of Acre?

12. What is the trade name for polytetrafluoroethylene?

13. Of what was the Zenith Lazy Bones an early example?

14. What was originally invented in 1935 for Jews who wouldn't operate machinery on the Sabbath?

15. In 2002, which food item did Danish scientists claim is more effective than grit for giving a grip on icy roads?

16. What did Frederick Walton invent after noticing that a skin forms on the top of paint?

17. Which acid is found in plain yoghurt?

18. What did Joseph Priestly invent in 1772 that has been ruining good whisky ever since?

19. What is the surname of the seven Italian brothers who developed a novel, bathroom use for agricultural pumps in 1955?

20. What was praised as THE invention of 2007 by Time magazine?

1. Who claimed he'd never met Hollywood madam Judy Babydoll Gibson, despite being named as a client of her sex parlour in her autobiography?

2. With whom did Julia Roberts cancel her wedding after rumours he'd had an affair with a stripper?

3. Who married Katie Holmes in a ceremony that was a compromise between Catholicism and Scientology?

4. Whose three-year relationship with Kate Winslet ended in 2001?

5. Who posed with the police number BK4454813 shortly before Divine Brown posed with BK4454822?

6. Which former wife of Brad Pitt reportedly had at least two nose jobs?

7. Who reportedly had Stella McCartney as matron of honour at her second wedding because Gwyneth Paltrow turned down the gig?

8. Who was engaged to, but never married, Sherilyn Fenn, Jennifer Grey and Winona Ryder?

9. Who moved in with Don Johnson when she was 14-years-old?

10. Who has been married to Patricia Arquette, Lisa Marie Presley and Alice Kim?

11. Which writer was divorced by Portuguese TV reporter Jorge Arantes?

12. What two-letter change did Johnny Depp have made to his 'Winona Forever' tattoo when they split?

13. Who did Mia Farrow claim would not go out to buy bed sheets without first consulting a psychiatrist?

14. Which fast-food chain did Robert Downey Jr claim had saved him from drug addiction?

15. Which pop diva was fired from a donut store for squirting jelly at customers?

16. Who passed out in a bathtub after eating a large helping of Tammy Wynette's peanut butter and banana pudding?

17. Which actress did Joan Rivers describe as having 'More chins than a Chinese telephone book'?

18. For how many days did Britney Spears' marriage to Jason Alexander last?

19. Who described the British royal family as a 'leper colony'?

20. Whose heterosexuality did Boy George call; 'The best kept secret in the music business'?

1. Where in the Royal Navy were women not permitted to serve until 2011?

2. Which meat product's six billionth can was sold in 2002?

3. Which was Britain's top-selling cask ale in 2019?

4. How many rows of kernels are there on the average corncob?

5. In which country do two-thirds of the world's kidnappings take place?

6. How did Abraham Lincoln's pet dog Fido die?

7. What is the most common name in nursery rhymes?

8. What was the only thing killed by the first Allied bomb dropped on Berlin in World War II?

9. What did Princess Diana get wrong during her wedding vows?

10. Which rock star was banned from South African radio after dedicating his 1985 Oscar to Nelson Mandela?

11. What is the only thing in the NATO phonetic alphabet that can be worn?

12. What has a sex discrimination board given male Norwegian soldiers the right to wear?

13. How many letters of the English language are used in Roman Numerals?

14. How many notes are there in two adjacent octaves?

15. What reason did Madonna claim for requesting a bottle of vodka in her dressing rooms?

16. What did BMW announce it would be the first company to produce cars without in 1991?

17. Which is the only Swedish word in the English language?

18. What was Brian's hometown in 'Monty Python's Life of Brian'?

19. In 1990, what did Oregon law make it illegal to be closer than two-feet to?

20. What has been illegal in London's Trafalgar Square since 2003?

1. Which was the world's first National Park?

2. Which river carved out the Grand Canyon?

3. Which man-made wonder does May Day parachute from when chased by James Bond in 'A View to a Kill'?

4. Which was the world's longest bridge when completed in 1937?

5. Which World Heritage Site in Jordan has been called 'A rose-red city half as old as time'?

6. Upon which river do the Dinka people rely for their existence?

7. Of which European country are Tahitians classed as citizens?

8. With what did the people of the Indonesian island of Sulawesi replace skulls when they gave up head hunting?

9. Which country attracts tourists to the Nazca Lines?

10. Which is the closest African country to the Canary Islands?

11. Which island's sacred sites include a temple devoted to one of Buddha's teeth?

12. Which is the world's largest container port?

13. Which German city is dubbed the Cradle of the Automobile?

14. What did Denmark lay claim to in 2014 that had previously been claimed by the U.S.A., Canada and Russia?

15. In which area of London will you find Bob Marley Way?

16. Which Italian island is famed for its Blue Grotto?

17. Which city is the main tourist attraction for cruise passengers landing in Piraeus?

18. Which country includes Africa's northernmost point?

19. Which is the world's smallest kingdom?

20. How many states make up the United Arab Emirates?

• •

1. What was the only international hit for Napoleon XIV?

2. What is everyone free to wear, according to Baz Luhrmann?

3. Who joined Peter Sellers on the hit record 'Goodness Gracious Me'?

4. Which Christmas song was a hit for the Singing Dogs?

5. What did Roger Miller sing you can't do in a buffalo herd?

6. Which comedy hit kept Ultravox's 'Vienna' from reaching the top of the U.K. singles chart?

7. Which hit by Boris Pickett and the Crypt-Kickers tends to be played on radio every Hallowe'en?

8. Who 'walks in the classroom cool and slow and who calls the English teacher Daddio'?

9. What animal was a hit for rockney stars Chas and Dave?

10. According to one of his biggest hits, what was Lonnie Donegan's old man?

11. What was Gordon, according to Jilted John?

12. Which character gave Rick Dees and his Cast of Idiots their biggest hit?

13. Which song begins: 'She was afraid to come out of the locker, she was nervous as she could be'?

14. What is the title of the Detergents' send-up of 'Leader of the Pack'?

15. Whose rendition of 'Tiptoe Through the Tulips' is on just about every list of great comedy records even if the singer always claimed he was being serious?

16. What was Chuck Berry's only U.K. chart-topper?

17. What did Loudon Wainwright III find lying in the middle of the road?

18. What does 'The Chicken Song' tell you to stick up your nose?

19. Which stand-up comedian had a hit with 'Elo John, Got a New Motor'?

20. Whose 'When I'm Cleaning Windows' was banned by the BBC?

1. What is SWATCH an abbreviation of?

2. Which pop diva went through a phase of encouraging girls to wear underwear as outerwear?

3. What flavour was the first batch of 'Two Dogs' alcopop?

4. Which name was given in the early 21st century to the shift by many UK shoppers to discount supermarkets?

5. Which fashion designer's bumsters were sometimes so low-slung as to be labelled 'virtually obscene'?

6. What were the G-1s that became fashion statements after featuring in 'Top Gun'?

7. Which facial fashion statement did Salma Hayek establish in the movie 'Frida'?

8. Which colour did your Mood Ring become if you left it in the freezer?

9. Which 1980s craze were invented by Xavier Roberts?

10. Which band's fans stole and wore VW badges?

11. What were newborn Cabbage Patch Kids called?

12. Which rapper pioneered the baggy pants look?

13. What might involve a six step, windmill, turtle and hand glide?

14. Which special day in 2004 saw Barbie split from Ken?

15. In the world of fashion what are Peter Pan and Fichu?

16. What took off in 1996 to be acclaimed the biggest dance craze since the Twist?

17. Which Indian premier gave his name to the collarless jackets sported by the Beatles?

18. During which year did the discovery of Tutankhamun's tomb spark a craze for all things Egyptian?

19. Which style joined the Levi jeans range in 1969?

20. Which greeting card and toy range gave birth to a TV show featuring Professor Coldheart?

1. In 1786, which punishment was Phoebe Harris the last person to suffer in the U.K.?

2. Which very famous family lost its final member when Jerome Napoleon died in 1945 from injuries incurred when he tripped over his dog's leash?

3. Who was the last Viceroy of India?

4. Who was the last of the Ptolemies to rule Egypt?

5. Who was the last British monarch unable to speak English?

6. Which title was Nicole Dunsdon the last to hold when her country banned it as degrading in 1991?

7. Which creature was last seen alive in 1681?

8. Which Simon and Garfunkel hit was the last song Elvis Presley performed in front of an audience?

9. Whose final words on the screen were: 'How do you find your way back in the dark'?

10. What is the link between the year 1900 and the sports of cricket, croquet, lacrosse and polo?

11. Which year saw Anne Frank's final diary entry?

12. In which year did Concorde make its final transatlantic flight?

13. How many days does a wonder last, according to the old proverb?

14. Who was the last man to set foot on the Moon?

15. Which movie's final words are: 'Oh no, it wasn't the airplanes. It was beauty killed the beast'?

16. Which was the last band to headline at the old Wembley Stadium?

17. Which is the last of Disney's Seven Dwarfs to leave the diamond mine when they sing 'Heigh Ho'?

18. Whose final words were: 'God damn the whole friggin' world and everyone in it but you, Carlotta'?

19. Who was Elizabeth Taylor's last husband?

20. What was the destination for the Monkees' 'Last Train'?

The Quizmaster's QUIZ BOOK

Tie Break Questions

• •

The closest to the answer wins.

Q. How many penalty goals were scored during the 2018 World Cup finals?

A. 22

Q. How many Munchkins appeared in the 1939 'Wizard of Oz' movie?

A. 132

Q. What's the total number of gifts in all the verses of 'The Twelve Days of Christmas'?

A. 364

Q. How many pints of salvia has the average human dribbled by the time of their first birthday?

A. 255

Q. How many teeth has a bear if it has a full set?

A. 42

Q. Yonge Street in Canada is listed in the Guinness Book of World Records as the world's longest street. How many miles long is Yonge Street?

A. 1,178 miles

Q. How many bones are there in a human foot?

A. 26

. . . .

Q. How many times its own weight does the average pet cat eat in a year?

A. Twenty eight times

Q. How many seats did the Tories lose in the May 2019 council elections?

A. 1,334

Q. What is the total if you add together all the numbers from one to one hundred?

A. 5050

Q. What percentage of prisoners in American jails are there for drug offences?

A. 55%

Q. What was the total length of the official Route 66 in miles?

A. 2,448 miles

Q. Amsterdam's foundations consist of timber piles driven into a bed of clay. How many timber piles are there?

A. 13,659

Q. How many gallons of wine does the average adult Italian consume in the average year?

A. 26

Q. China's longest river is the Yangtze, how many miles long is it?

A. 3,494 miles

Q. At the start of 2015, how many people in England and Wales claimed Cornish as their first language?

A. 557

Q. Wembley claims to have more toilets than any other stadium in the world, how many?

A. 2,618

Q. How many miles of motorway were there in the U.K. at the start of 2016?

A. 2,173

Q. How tall is Nelson's Column from the bottom of the pedestal to the top of Nelson's hat?

A. 51.6 metres or 169 feet 3 inches

Q. How many feet of nose hair does the average human grow in an average lifetime?

A. Six

Q. What was the population of India at the start of 2015?

A. 1,660,079,217

Q. How many calories are burnt up by a 60 second passionate kiss?

A. 26

Q. How many words in the English language end with the letters 'dous'?

A. Four (hazardous, horrendous, stupendous, tremendous)

· ·

Q. How many steps are there from the bottom to the top of the Eiffel Tower?

A. 1,792

Q. To the nearest ten million, how many sheep are there in New Zealand?

A. 70 million

Q: How many stitches hold together the average soccer ball?

A: 642

Q. How many more bones has an adult horse than an adult human?

A. 18

Q. In kilometres, what is the diameter of the Moon?

A. 3,476km

Q. How old was Isaac Newton when he discovered the Law of Gravity?

A. 23

Q. What percentage of food consumed in the USA is dairy products?

A. 29%

The Quizmaster's QUIZ BOOK

Answers

. . . .

ONE - HUMAN NATURE: 1. Nail biting 2. Nails 3. Stockholm Syndrom
4. Eyelids 5. Cyst 6. Syphilis 7. 14% 8. Rumbling stomach 9. Bunic
10. Soap 11. Hair 12. Twice as big 13. 50% 14. In pubs 15. Lavatory 1
Cut their own hair 16. In the eyes 18. Vomiting 19. Finger or toenai
20. Sweat

TWO – LIFESTYLE: 1. Elizabeth Arden's 2. Toys R Us 3. 3-D movies
John Batterson Stetson 5. Sesame seeds 6. Twelve 7. Root beer 8. Hube
9. Sherry 10. Keeper 11. London Fog 12. Green Giant 13. A champagr
or sparkling wine cork 14. Krispy Kreme Donuts 15. Hard Rock Café 1
Gucci 16. Napoleon 17. Hunter Wellington boots 19. Michael Jacksc
20. Yarg is Gray backwards. (The nettle wrapped Cornish cheese takes i
name from the company founders Alan and Jenny Gray,)

THREE – HISTORY: 1. Dream 2. Broadway 3. Edward VII 4. Communit
Service 5. London Lord Mayor's Show 6. His rifle 7. Trial by jury
Victoria 9. Monaco 10. Eight 11. Pope (Pope John Paul I)12. Charles
13. Gerald Ford 14. Bill Clinton 15. Sheep farm 16. Pauline Wayne wa
his pet cow 17. Pennsylvania (Spelt Pensylvania which was one of sever
accepted spellings at the time) 18. Helen of Troy 19. Calamity Jar
20. Elizabeth I

FOUR – POP AND ROCK OLDIES: 1. Pink Floyd's 'The Dark Sic
of the Moon' 2. Edison 3. Bill Haley and the Comets 4. Joan Chandc
Baez 5. Greta Garbo 6. 'Blowin' in the Wind' 7. Zero. Presley's manage
Tom Parker released the album of Elvis chatting between songs to avo
paying royalties on the music. 8. 'Ain't No Sunshine' 9. 'I Just Called t
Say I Love You' 10. The Highwaymen 11. Spinal Tap 12. Spider Murph
13. Jerry Lee Lewis 14. Cher 15. Houston 16. Cadillac 17. 'Arthu
18. Bass guitar 19. London 20. Bruce Springsteen

FIVE – SPORTS: 1. Belgium 2. Badminton racket 3. Drama in Baham
(Trevor Berbick beat Ali on a unanimous points decision at the 1981 figl
in Nassau) 4. Trinidad and Tobago 5. Claret jug 6. Eight 7. Horsesho
pitching 8. Four 9. Bind 10. Chris Evert 11. Golf 12. Volleyball 1.
Baseball 14. Homer Simpson 15. Roleo 16. The speed of a putting gree
17. Triple bagel 18. Venus Williams 19. Jack Nicklaus 20. Basketball

• •

SIX – MUSICALS AND CLASSICAL MUSIC: 1. 'Grease' 2. 'Dance of the Hours' 3. 'Hairspray' 4. Dover 5. 'High Society' 6. 'Staying Alive' 7. 'Das Rheingold' 8. 'Carousel' 9. 'A Chorus Line' 10. 'Hair' the show was just three performances short of its 2,000 mark.11. 'Baby It's Cold Outside' (Tom Jones was joined by Cerys Matthews on the hit recording) 12. Glenn Miller 13. 'The Gay Divorcee' 14. 110 15. Beethoven 16. Ninth 17. 'Hustle and Flow' 18. 'Afternoon' 19 Edward Elgar 20. 'Matilda'

SEVEN – OLYMPICS: 1. Taekwondo 2. Five 3. The Flying Tomato 4. 800m 5. Izzy 6. Table tennis 7. High jump 8. 30 seconds 9. A Japanese flag 10. Banana 11. Four 12. The Pringle 13. Searle 14. Nobel Peace Prize 15. First black Olympian 16. All measurements were in yards rather than metres 17. India 18. Four (Despite never actually changing nationality she competed in six Olympics under the flags of Yugoslavia, Independent Olympic Participants, Serbia and Montenegro and Serbia)19. Tennis (She won the title in 1900) 20. Football (soccer)

EIGHT - THE WRITTEN WORD: 1. 'The Mouse That Roared' 2. Gulliver 3. Mr Pickwick 4. White 5. Snow (It is the last snowy day of the winter) 6. Dixon 7. 'Adam Bede' 8. 'King Ralph' 9. 'Midnight Cowboy' 10. Phoenix 11. Buck Rogers 12. Clock 13. T.H. White 14. 'The Love Bug' 15. Nevada 16. 'In the Heat of the Night' 17. Harry Potter 18. Church 19. Alibi 20. 'Black Beauty'

NINE - ART AND ARTISTS: 1. Jeff Koons 2. Yellow 3. The Peace Sign 4. Theatre 5. Man Ray 6. Vincent van Gogh 7. 19th 8. Florence 9. Aubrey Beardsley 10. He dropped the H from Breughel 11. Painter 12. Photographs 13. Painting 14. Enamel (accept glass) 15. American 16. Caricatures 17. Salvador Dali 18. Uncle and nephew 19. Boxing 20. Edouard Manet's

TEN - MOVIES: 1. Grunt 2. 'Dr Strangelove' 3. 'Moonstruck' 4. Clint Eastwood 5. Good Guy 6. Ray Stanz 7. 'Live and Let Die' 8. 'Star Wars' (The jazzy 'Cantina Song' was composed by John Williams.) 9. Al's Toy Barn 10. The Dirty Dozen 11. 'Do' 12. Ziggy Marley 13. 'Home Alone' 14. Dog Years 15. 'American Graffiti' 16 Henderson 17. Dot Matrix 18. Kermit the Frog, (He names this in 'The Muppet Movie') 19. 'A Tale of Two Cities 20. The Joker

· ·

ELEVEN - TV: 1. Oscar the Grouch 2. Placido Flamingo 3. Double Crunch 4. Dixie 5. Dracula 6. Snagglepus 7. 'Battlestar Galactica' 8. The Beverley Hillbillies 9. The Partridge Family 10. 'Taxi' 11. Angus 12. Cobblestone County 13. Blush 14. Cleopatra 15. 'ALF' 16. Doug 17. Xena's horse 18. Dead Dog Records 19. 'Mighty Morphin' Power Rangers' 20. Columbo

TWELVE - IT'S ONLY HUMAN: 1. Writer's cramp 2. The front teeth 3. Nose bleed 4. Double vision 5. Headache 6. Jet lag 7. Smell 8. Runny nose 9. It's a fear of animal fur 10. Bulls 11. The heart 12. Cheek bone 13. Back of the knees 14. Ears 15. Clogged drains 16. Optic nerve 17. Smell 18. Congestive heart failure 19. Kidney 20. Chicken

THIRTEEN - THE NATURAL WORLD: 1. Horse 2. Four 3. Longest gestation period (up to 38 months) 4. Rat 5. Lower shell 6. Teeth 7. Grape 8. Cat 9. Twice as fast 10. Gout 11. Bee 12. Banana 13. Badger 14. Condor 15. Shrewdness 16. Alligator 17. Camel 18. Nepal 19. Five 20. A fish

FOURTEEN - SCIENCE AND INVENTIONS: 1. The shopping trolley 2. Water displacement 3. Thirteen 4. Whistle 5. Isuzu 6. TV remote control 7. Hubble length (it is equivalent to 13.8 billion light years) 8. Mercury 9. ae 10. Resonance 11. Sodium (was known as natrium) 12. 21 13. Whitewash 14. Antacid 15. Home (Video Home System) 16. Wolfram 17. Saint Dominic 18. Diptheria 19. 20 (Six were built for development and 14 for commercial service) 20. Lightning

FIFTEEN - FAMOUS PEOPLE: 1. H Norman Schwarzkopf 2. Kevin Spacey Fowler's 3. Bette Midler 4. Archbishop of York 5. Pope John Pal II (The album reached 175 on the Billboard album chart) 6. Prince Andrew, Duke of York. 7. Margaret 8. 40 9. A payphone 10. Flying 11. Tiger 12. Twins 13. Her legs 14. Buddhism 15. Arizona 16. Oxford 17. Aquarius 18. India 19. Popes 20. 50

SIXTEEN - MIXED BAG: 1. On a U.S. dollar bill 2. Arlene 3. Salvation Army 4. Dolls 5. Brown 6. Three 7. Three 8. Three 9. Alexandria 10. Lizards 11. December 12. Pegasus 13. Grated horseradish 14. Gold 15. 150 years 16. Lifeboat 17. Exclamation mark! 18. Cedar 19. Hell 20. Easel

• •

SEVENTEEN - GAMES: 1. Gin Rummy 2. Nine 3. 24 4. 50 5. Clyde 6. Othello 7. Boardwalk 8. Harvest Moon 9. The Millennium Falcon spaceship 10. TILT 11. Bono 12. Scrabble 13. Clubs 14. Zero – there is no such rule 15. Blackjack 16. Ten 17. Britain 18. Three 19. Contract Bridge 20. Chess

EIGHTEEN - WORLD TRAVEL: 1. Windsor Castle 2. It is also noon in Lisbon 3. French Sudan 4. Sixth 5. Amsterdam 6. Reno 7. Acapulco 8. Olive branches 9. Santa Ana 10. Morocco 11. Cairo 12. Adriatic 13. Euro 14. Blue 15. Saudi Arabia 16. Gulf of Guinea 17. The Alps 18. Beijing 19. Thailand 20. Miami Beach

NINETEEN - STAIRWAY TO HEAVEN - WHO DIED WHEN?: 1. Robert Kennedy 1968 2. Dwight D. Eisenhower 1969 3. 1970 4. 1973 5. 1977 6. 1978 7. 1979 8. John Lennon 1980 9. Bob Marley 1981 10. 1985 11. Rudolf Hess 1987 12. 1989 13. 1991 14. 1992 15. 1993 16. 1994 17. Princess Diana 1997 18. 1998 19. 2001 20. Maurice Gibb 2003

TWENTY - WORLD HISTORY: 1. Edward II 2. George Washington 3. Crete 4. 1920s 5. 1990s 6. France 7. 1990s (1993) 8. Sugar (prior to this it had been cotton and tobacco) 9. Botswana 10. B.P. (British Petroleum) 11. French 12. Brazil 13. Ecuador (He moved into the London Ecuadorian Embassy in 2012) 14. Honduras 15. Auschwitz 16. Axis Sally (The radio propaganda slots were filled by American Mildred Elizabeth Gillars and Italian American Rita Zucca)17. Five 18. Sir Francis Drake 19. He robbed banks (he was also involved with kidnapping and ransom demands) 20. Richard Nixon

TWENTY-ONE - FASHION: 1. Hair styles 2. Lotus shoes 3. Knees 4. Vanity sizing 5. Hermes 6. London 7. Gap (known as The Gap by some in America) 8. The bra strap clip 9. Black and white 10. Clicking the heels three times 11. A hat 12. Red 13. Socks 14. Naked lady tattoos 15. Queen Victoria's 16. Neck ties 17. Playtex – yes that's right, the bra company 18. The Lacoste crocodile – it is not an alligator 19. Jay Z 20. New York (Usually held in February then another in September)

TWENTY-TWO - FOOD AND DRINK: 1. Seven 2. An olive 3. China 4. Mount Vesuvius 5. Boar's head 6. Schlitz 7. Herbs (Americans are often surprised to hear Brits pronounce the letter 'H' at the start of 'herbs. Brits are surprised when Americans miss it out.) 8. Nutmeg 9. Daiquiri 10. Southern Comfort 11. Tia Moo Moo 12. Pigeon 13. Doughnut (or Donut if you're American) 14. Kentucky 15. Paella (Despite claims in some sources it is not an Arabic word for 'leftovers')16. Beaujolais Nouveau 17. Austria 18. Walnuts 19. Perrier Water 20. Roquefort

TWENTY-THREE - POP MUSIC: 1. Stars 2. Kid Rock 3. Arctic Monkeys 4. Michael Jackson 5. 'Yellow' 6. R. Kelly 7. Lorde 8. Scissor Sisters 9. 'Gorilla' 10. Lou Rawls 11. Troyal Garth Brooks' 12. Greta Garbo 13. Melanie Chisholm – Mel C – Sporty 14. 'Four Weddings and a Funeral' (Originally recorded by the Troggs and written by their singer Reg Presley. The Wet Wet Wet version from the movie topped the U.K. chart for 15 consecutive weeks and Reg said he'd spend his royalty windfall on research into crop circles.) 15. REM 16. 'The Sound of Music' ('With the Beatles' was the second) 17. 'Don't Shoot Me I'm Only the Piano Player' 18. Barbra Streisand's 19. The sky – clouds 20. Bob Dylan

TWENTY-FOUR - SPORTS TERMS: 1. Dolly 2. Commence fighting 3. Archery 4. Wind direction 5. Go 6. Centre forward 7. Zero 8. Sailing 9. The grid of lines 10. Practice balls 11. Boxing (Anyone who fancied his chances in a bout could challenge the boxer by throwing his hat in the ring) 12. His head 13. A practice arrow 14. Par five 15. Cock fighting 16. Angler 17. Sumo wrestling 18. Beach volleyball 19. To the referee 20. Abseiling

TWENTY-FIVE - STAGE AND MOVIE MUSICALS: 1. 'Let the Sun Shine In' 2. 'My Fair Lady' 3. 'The Music Man' 4. Hi-Spot 5. Hurricanes 6. 'I Remember It Well' 7. 'Bedknobs and Broomsticks' 8. 'Seven Brides for Seven Brothers' (Pontipee is the surname of the brothers and their future brides) 9. Tess 10. 2001 Odyssey 11. Yellow 12. 'After Midnight' (After using conventional uppercase initials and later with no punctuation, at the time of writing k.d. lang is lowercase with full-stops (periods) after her initials) 13. 'Motown: The Musical' 14. 'Matilda: The Musical' 15. 'Kinky Boots' 16. 'Cinderella' 17. Bono and The Edge 18. 'Sister Act' 19. Cole Porter's 20. 'Priscilla, Queen of the Desert'

• •

TWENTY-SIX - BOOKS AND BOOKMEN: 1. Cecil Day-Lewis 2. 'Little Red Riding Hood' 3. Ace 4. Ahmed 5. Albatross 6. The length of time Robinson Crusoe was marooned on the island 7. 33 8. William Shakespeare 9. 'Die Hard 2' 10. Noel Coward 11. Tom (despite what anyone else might have told you) 12. Phileas Fogg 13. 'Breakfast at Tiffany's' 14. Scarlett O'Hara 15. Cherry Tree Lane (home of the Banks family in 'Mary Poppins') 16. April 17. A woman 18. York 19. A mouse 20. Boxing

TWENTY-SEVEN - ALL ABOUT ART: 1. Moscow's (It hangs in the Pushkin Museum) 2. It was painted out of doors 3. Patination or verdigris 4. In a church 5. Art Deco 6. Fish 7. Michelangelo 8. Edgar 9. World War I 10. Action painting 11. Water 12. Textiles 13. Damien Hirst 14. Florence's 15. Mark Rothco 16. Rene Magritte 17. Hermann Goring 18. The big toe 19. He suffered from cataracts 20. Amsterdam's

TWENTY-EIGHT - SILVER SCREEN : 1. Camp Mohawk 2. 'Dick Tracy' 3. Buster 4. Harry and Sally 5. 'Indiana Jones and the Temple of Doom' (The club is a homage to 'Star Wars' which was also produced by George Lucas and starred Harrison Ford) 6. Club 69 7. Performing dolphins 8. Bambi and Thumper 9. 'Batman Returns' 10. 'The Seven Year Itch' 11. Daily Paper 12. 'Jailhouse Rock' 13. Ten thousand 14. Kris Kringle ('Miracle on 34th Street') 15. The Black Widows 16. Blue Oyster 17. Blue 18. Mr Bigglesworth 19. Two 20. Guns (He steals three of them)

TWENTY-NINE - SMALL SCREEN: 1. The Addams Family 2. Time (One bleem equals a year) 3. A bee 4. Amanda 5. 'Diff'rent Strokes' 6. Jennifer Lopez 7. Captain Link Hogthrob 8. Ron Howard 9. James K. Polk High School 10. Edna 11. Krusty Krab 12. Lady Bird 13. Loupone 14. Penrod Pooch 15. The Simpsons 16. Pork 17. They are all set in towns called Springfield 18. Wanker 19. Spike 20. Brian Griffin

THIRTY - ALL ABOUT YOUR BODY : 1. Ears (It is the technical term for earwax) 2. Eight 3. Arthritis 4. Eyes 5. Tongue 6. Cold sore 7. Old books 8. Air 9. Twenty percent 10. Hives 11. A toilet 12. Mud 13. Kidneys 14. Sweat glands 15. Six months prior to birth 16. Legionaire's disease 17. Head lice infestation 18. Impetigo 19. Wisdom tooth 20. August

. . . .

THIRTY-ONE - WILDLIFE : 1. Rats 2. Abdomen 3. Worms 4. Once a year 5. Starfish (The Crown of Thorns Starfish to be precise) 6. Amazon 7. Water 8. Cod 9. Seaweed 10. Albatross 11. Ear 12. Chatter 13. Walrus 14. Raven 15. Duck 16. Two 17. Five 18. One 19. Crocodile 20. Eight

THIRTY-TWO - SCIENCE YOU PROBABLY DIDN'T LEARN AT SCHOOL : 1. February 2. He always put on the right shoe first 3. 1940s 4. Flying saucer 5. 1940s (1948) 6. Astronomy 7. Apollo 9 8. Sixteenth century 9. Flotsum 10. World War II 11. Polish 12. Olive oil 13. Twenty 14. 1930s 15. Credit or debit card 16. 1900s 17. Japan 18. 1920s (1928) 19. Bridges 20. Tank

THIRTY-THREE CELEBS ANCIENT AND MODERN: 1. Elton John 2. Mick Hucknall 3. In a plane crash 4. Donald Trump 5. Michelin 6. Ronald Reagan 7. David Niven 8. Thomas Edison 9. Olivia Newton-John's 10. The Who 11. Five 12. Hungarian 13. A bowl of water 14. Madonna 15. Memphis 16. Neil Armstrong 17. Linda Evans 18. Ozzy Osbourne 19. Smoking a cigar 20. She jumped from the H of the Hollywood sign

THIRTY-FOUR - BITS AND PIECES: 1. Tea drinking 2. Salt Lake City 3. A boat (Propelled by a sail and/or oars, once used throughout the Mediterranean but now seen almost exclusively on the Nile) 4. Buddhism 5. Tines 6. Job Centre 7. Ballet 8. Lent 9. 'What will be will be' 10. Noon 11. North 12. Clean the tracks 13. Queen Victoria's 14. All cats 15. Fifteen 16. Aquarius 17. Coffee 18. Treason 19. A voice 20. 'Happy Birthday'

THIRTY-FIVE - POT LUCK : 1. He saw Diana bathing naked 2. Toilet paper 3. Five 4. The Promised Land 5. The rear mast 6. England 7. An Irish mountain range 8. Duty Free Shop (Opened in 1947) 9. Palm Sunday 10. The White Hart 11. L plates for learners 12. Israel 13. Three (Tuk tuks are a cheap form of transport in the East, especially India, known as auto rickshaws) 14. Z (He was Zorro) 15. Kill 16. Australia 17. Electric lighting 18. Sen 19. The Bull's Head 20. Three

THIRTY-SIX - INDOOR GAMES : 1. Two 2. 23 3. Craps 4. Seventeen 5. Chess 6. Chess ratings. Named after chess master Arpad Elo. 7. Monopoly 8. Darts 9. Marbles 10. Land areas 11. Cranium 12. Jenga 13. The Monopoly prisoner 14. Bingo 15. Tungsten 16. Mars 17. Yellow 18. The bar 19. Cribbage 20. Atari

• •

THIRTY-SEVEN - AROUND THE WORLD: 1. Bethlehem 2. Addis Ababa 3. Kabul 4. Benin 5. Three 6. Cape Verdi 7. Peru 8. Three (Yangtze, Yellow and Huai also known as the Pearl River) 9. Colombia 10. Costa Rica 11. Cuba 12. Leeds 13. Czech Republic 14. Denmark 15. Denmark 16. Dominican Republic 17. Lisbon 18. Roman Catholic 19. Black 20. A tree (Silk cotton tree)

THIRTY-EIGHT - BACK IN TIME : 1. Ronald Reagan 2. Italy 3. Peanut 4. Breadfruit trees 5. France 6. Sir Francis Drake 7. Spain's 8. Cambodia 9. London 10. Nicholas II 11. Adolf Hitler 12. France 13. Omaha 14. Spam 15. Soviet Union 16. The English Channel 17. Kneeling in prayer 18. Eliot Ness 19. Fifth birthday 20. Richard Nixon

THIRTY-NINE - GETTING TRENDY: 1. Katy Perry's 2. Paris 3. 'Chanel No 5' 4. Marc Jacobs' 5. Dr Martens boots 6. Shoes with a blue sole 7. Marc Jacobs 8. Rose and jasmine 9. Pulse points 10. 'Aramis' 11. Florence 12. Shoes 13. 'Armani' 14. Picasso 15. Elizabeth Taylor 16. Nina Ricci 17. Yves St Laurent (Accept YSL) 18. Thomas 19. 'Ultimo' 20. Hugo Boss

FORTY - ROCK 'N' POP: 1. 'One Night' 2. The I-Three 3. Bernie Taupin 4. Nelly ('Herre' is correct spelling) 5. Beyonce Knowles (Accept Beyonce) 6. Alicia Keys' 7. Christina Aguilera's 8. Savage Garden 9. 'High Voltage' 10. Whitney Houston's 11. The Rolling Stones 12. Eminem (The other half was Royce Da 5'9") 13. 'Boy' 14. 'Piano Man' 15. Aerosmith 16. Zero 17. Baseball 18. 'Brothers in Arms' 19. Metallica 20. Beyonce Knowles (Accept Beyonce)

FORTY-ONE - SPORTS AND SPORTS PEOPLE: 1. Pete Sampras 2. Five 3. 1950s (1954) 4. The North Sea 5. Angelique Kerber 6. Alexander Graham Bell 7. 'Octopussy' 8. Twenty four 9. Lacrosse stick 10. Five 11. Red balls 12. Tennis dress 13. Argentina 14. Costa Rica 15. February 16. He swam under water 17. Davis Cup 18. Mo Farah 19. 30th 20. Four

FORTY-TWO - MUSICAL THEATRE: 1. 'Rain' 2. 'Promises, Promises' 3. Green Day 4. 'La Cage Aux Folles' 5. 'A Little Night Music' 6. Memphis 7. 'Next to Normal' 8. 'Rock of Ages' 9. 'Hair' 10. 'West Side Story' 11. 'Shrek: The Musical' 12. 'Billy Elliot' 13. 'Sunday in the Park with George' 14. 'The Little Mermaid' 15. 'Grease' 16. 'Young Frankenstein' 17. 'Legally Blonde' 18. 'Tarzan' 19. 'The Wedding Singer' 20. Bert

• •

FORTY-THREE - OLYMPIC FIRSTS : 1. Pyeongchang 2018 2. A pool, (They had previously swum in lakes or rivers) 3. Japan 4. 1912 5. The Olympic Oath 6. Paris 7. The 400m-long track 8. Alcohol 9. First woman to light the flame 10. Dachshund 11. 1980 12. Cathy Freeman (Sydney in 2000) 13. Ethiopia 14. Rome 15. Beijing 16. Usain Bolt 17. Romania 18. Red and yellow cards 19. Melbourne 20. 2004

FORTY-FOUR - NOVEL BEGINNINGS: 1. 'Babbitt' 2. 'The Bell Jar' (Sylvia Plath) 3. 'Brave New World' 4. 'The Bridges of Madison County' 5. Newspapers 6. 'Candide' 7. 'Carrie' 8. 'The Catcher in the Rye' 9. 'It was love at first sight' 10. 'Charlotte's Web' 11. Marley's 12. 'The Color Purple' 13. July 14. 'A Farewell to Arms' 15. 'Foundation' 16. 'Jane Eyre' (by Charlotte) 17. 'Jurassic Park' 18. 'Little Women' 19. Hudson 20. Mole

FORTY-FIVE - SITTING IN THE BACK ROW: 1. Six 2. Popeye 3. It's his I.Q. 4. Cigarette lighter 5. Abandoned Planet 6. Charlton Heston 7. Danny DeVito 8. Anthony Hopkins 9. Batman 10. Fleur-de-Lis 11. David Bowie 12. Six 13. Peter Pan 14. Emilio Largo 15. 'Strangers on a Train' 16. 'The Sword in the Stone' 17. 'Pulp Fiction' 18. 'The Blair Witch Project' 19. 'The Temple of Doom' 20. 'Million Dollar Baby'

FORTY-SIX - COUCH POTATOES: 1. Moe (An extra point for anyone who knows his surname is Szyslak) 2. Summers 3. Slugger 4. 'Breaking Bad' (Walter White in the original) 5. Seven 6. Barney Stinson 7. Seinfeld 8. Baltimore 9. 'Six Feet Under' 10. Martin Luther King Jr. 11. Stoneway 12. Oprah Winfrey 13. 'Doctor Who' 14. Brazil 15. William Shatner (Kissing Nichelle Nichols on 'Star Trek') 16. Red 17. Oliver Queen 18. The White House 19. Dublin 20. 'Teenage Mutant Ninja Turtles'

FORTY-SEVEN - ONE WORLD: 1. The Taj Mahal 2. The Leaning Tower of Pisa 3. Five (The same five vowels as in English) 4. Four (Australia, Fiji, New Zealand and Tuvalu) 5. Calvados 6. Ganges 7. Malaysia 8. Tel Aviv 9. John F. Kennedy International Airport 10. Ireland 11. Stromboli 12. Quebec 13. Cyprus 14. Camp David 15. Tigris 16. Krakatoa 17. Champs-Elysees 18. Brooklyn 19. The Bahamas (Nassau) 20. Harrods

FORTY-EIGHT - FLORA AND FAUNA: 1. Yellow 2. A stem 3. Fish 4. They squeak 5. Tree 6. Lions 7. Camel's milk 8. Penguin 9. Avocado 10. Muscles 11. Yellow 12. Zero 13. Cretaceous 14. Five 15. Chromosomes

ANSWERS

16. Petals 17. Broadcast 18. Ants or termites 19. After rain 20. Goat

FORTY-NINE - SIMPLY SCIENCE : 1. Lung capacity 2. Blue 3. Genetics 4. Sugar 5. It landed in the dark 6. Sea water 7. Dye (To remain in the cloth dye has to be fixed) 8. The letter 'S' consisting of three dots 9. The world's first powered flight took place in Chard in 1848, some 55 years before the Wright Brothers 10. PET 11. Witch hazel 12. Glass 13. 1930s 14. Volkswagen 15. One-third 16. Video 17. Stereo sound 18. Montgolfier 19. Water 20. Dreamliner

FIFTY - PEOPLE IN THE PAST: 1. Rock Hudson 2. Louis-Philippe 3. Austrian 4. Groucho Marx 5. Muhammad's 6. Fanny Adams (aka Sweet Fanny Adams) 7. Oil 8. Winston Churchill 9. William the Conqueror 10. Henry II 11. Physics 12. Mahatma Gandhi 13. Independence Day 14. H.G. Selfridge 15. They made violins 16. Queen Victoria 17. He wore a kilt 18. Charlotte (Anne died aged 29, Emily aged 30 and Charlotte 38) 19. William Blake 20. Portugal

FIFTY-ONE VIDEO GAMES: 1. First Person Shooter 2. 'Call of Duty' 3.'Pac-Man' 4. '007 – Licence to Kill' 5. 'The House of the Dead' 6. 'A Boy and his Blob' 7. The Visitors Centre 8. The crown 9. David Bowie 10. Princess Zelda 11. Street racing 12. The Caribbean 13. 'Mortal Kombat' 14. 'Nintendogs' 15. 'Phantasy Star' 16. 'Pokemon' 17. Merlin 18. 'Dungeons and Dragons' 19. 'Doom' 20. Pigs

FIFTY-TWO - PASSPORT TIME: 1. Vermont 2. Lake District 3. Cuba 4. It is shaped like an eel 5. A bell 6. River Nile 7. Adriatic Sea 8. Barcelona 9. Balearic Islands 10. Poland 11. Portugal 12. The Limpopo 13. Mesa 14. The Strip 15. St Paul's Cathedral 16. Borneo 17. Munich's 18. Marble 19. Switzerland 20. S

FIFTY-THREE - GOING BACK: 1. Mi Lai 2. Homosexuality 3. Kobe 4. George VI 5. Apache 6. They carried his library 7. Pacific 8. Hail 9. Spain 10. Hanging at the yard-arm 11. Good Friday 12. Iraq 13. 30-years war 14. Manchester 15. Sunday (remembered as Bloody Sunday) 16. Rudolf Hess 17. Turkey 18. Treason 19. Mother's Day (The much older Mothering Sunday observed in Britain was originally a Christian event celebrating the Mother Church) 20. Liverpool

FIFTY-FOUR - IN ITS FASHION : 1. Black 2. Hot pants 3. Pierre Cardin
4. Demi Moore 5. 'Frankie Say Relax' (Note: the middle word is SAY, not
SAYS) 6. Vivienne Westwood 7. Zip fasteners 8. Sting 9. Furbish 10. Levi
Strauss 11. His use of fox fur 12. Paris 13. Revlon 14. 'Galliano Girl' 15.
Capri pants 16. Queen Elizabeth II 17. Saks of Fifth Avenue 18. Armani
19. Rene Lacoste 20. Calvin Klein

FIFTY-FIVE - EAT, DRINK AND BE MERRY: 1. Aberdeen 2. Five (The
hats are known as toques) 3. Mexico 4. Japan's 5. Cheeses 6. Sicily 7.
Denmark 8. Chicken 9. Bremen 10. Bordeaux 11. Turkey 12. A brand of
beer 13. Curry 14. Holland 15. Pepsi-Cola 16. Stella Artois 17. Anchovy
18. Nougat 19. Saffron 20. Advocaat

FIFTY-SIX - JUKE BOX: 1. Bon Jovi 2. 'Chiquitita' 3. Stormzy 4. Guns n'
Roses 5. Prince 6. The E Street Band 7. Kanye West 8. George Michael 9.
Def Leppard 10. 'Sixteen' 11. Donna Summer 12. Three 13. Barry White
14. Lady Gaga 15. Bruno Mars 16. 'The Monster is Loose' 17. Tom Petty
18. The Black Eyed Peas 19. Tupac Shakur 20. Three

FIFTY-SEVEN - SPORTS RULES, GEAR & PRIZES: 1. Bamboo 2. 1930
(1934) 3. Powerboat racing 4. World's best soccer goalkeeper 5. White 6.
Golf club 7. Puma 8. Table tennis 9. Tea 10. Golf (A feathery was a ball
made from leather stuffed with feathers) 11. Bisque 12. Lewis Hamilton
13. Britain 14. Football (Soccer) 15. Golf 16. Zero 17. Steffi Graf 18.
Poker World Series 19. Curling 20. 100%

FIFTY-EIGHT - THE GREAT WHITE WAY: 1. 'The Color Purple' 2.
'Jersey Boys' 3. 'Dirty Rotten Scoundrels' 4. 'Wicked' 5. 'Avenue Q' 6.
'The Times They Are A-Changing' 7. Dame Judi Dench 8. 'Hairspray'
9. 'Mamma Mia' 10. Paris' 11. Pigeon breeding 12. There were no actual
musicians in the theatre, the score was entirely recorded 13. 'Aida' 14.
'Annie Get Your Gun' 15. 'Footloose' 16. 'Beauty and the Beast' 17.
'The Circle of Life' 18. 'Jekyll and Hyde' 19. 'Victor/Victoria' 20. 'Sunset
Boulevard'

FIFTY-NINE - GOLD, SILVER, BRONZE: 1. A snowball 2. 2016
(The Rio Games took place in August and Brazilian winter is from

• •

June to September) 3. Australasia 4. BMX 5. Zero 6. Coffee 7. For not entering any competitors 8. Eric Moussambani was dubbed Eric the Eel 9. Liechtenstein 10. Iran (He was a boxer) 11. Sweden 12. Underwater photographers 13. Montreal 1976 14. Sections of the torch relay 15. Players who had taken part in a World Cup 16. Skeleton 17. Micronesia 18. Namibia 19. Nigeria 20. Qatar

SIXTY - POPULAR FICTION: 1. Shaving equipment 2. 'The Wizard of Oz' 3. Tara (In 'Gone with the Wind') 4. 'Second Foundation' 5. 'The Red Pony' 6. A lake 7. 'The Hitchhiker's Guide to the Galaxy' 8. Bathilda Bagshot 9. 'War of the Worlds' 10. His cutlass 11. Katie 12. 'She' 13. Laughing water 14. 'Leather Stocking' 15. Willy Wonka 16. 'Bambi' 17. Scarlet fever 18. 'The Life and Adventures of Nicholas Nickleby' 19. Garfield 20. 'Dune'

SIXTY-ONE - OLD AND NEW MOVIES: 1. Italics 2. 'GoldenEye' 3. Jawas 4. Mr Jingles 5. Doc Brown's children 6. 'Black Panther' 7. A Polka Band 8. Khartoum 9. A mini helicopter 10. 'Big' 11. Dean Martin and Jerry Lewis 12. Max 13. Middlesex 14. Austin Powers 15. Moby Dick 16. Moon 17. 'Butch Cassidy and the Sundance Kid' 18. Mount Rose 19. Mr Smileys 20. 'Blazing Saddles'

SIXTY-TWO - ON THE BOX: 1. 'Game of Thrones' 2. Sherlock Holmes 3. Junior 4. Tony Blair 5. 'South Park' 6. Richard E. Grant 7. Six 8. 'Sorry we are closed' 9. A single mother 10. Po 11. Monica's apartment 12. 'Twin Peaks' 13. The Den 14. Ned Flanders 15. Six 16. Father Jack (from the TV series 'Father Ted') 17. Norah Jones 18. 'Absolutely Fabulous' 19. Suzi Quatro 20. Salem

SIXTY-THREE - LAND AND SEA CREATURES: 1. Windy weather (Wind annoys bees and makes them more aggressive) 2. Three 3. One 4. Running on water 5. Otter 6. Bubbles 7. They have no jaws 8. A duck 9. Webbed feet 10. Thirteen 11. A sheep 12. Locust 13. Yellow 14. Hearts 15. Wasp 16. Vocal sounds 17. A shark can blink both eyes at the same time 18. Eyes 19. Pig 20.Bats

SIXTY-FOUR - SCI-FACTS: 1. Abraham Lincoln 2. Yellow 3. Aluminium (or aluminum if you're American) 4. The dentist's drill 5. Copper

• •

6. Osmium 7. Eight 8. Columbia 9. Two 10. Length 11. Japan 12. Lime 13. The H-bomb 14. Lakes 15. Four 16. Tin 17. Cells 18. Amphibians 19. Nine times brighter 20. Pathfinder

SIXTY-FIVE - NOTHING STRANGER THAN FOLK: 1. Benito Mussolini 2. Sadian 3. Black London taxi 4. Gossip 5. Sug (Selling under guise) 6. Payess 7. Miss World 8. Greece 9. Paul Simon 10. Boris Yeltsin 11. Margaret Thatcher 12. Geri Halliwell (Ginger) (Victoria Beckham became a Goodwill Ambassador in 2014) 13. Two 14. David Arquette 15. Prince William 16. Jude Law 17. Glenn Miller 18. Michael Jackson 19. Prince Philip the Duke of Edinburgh 20. Catherine Zeta-Jones

SIXTY-SIX - ROUTE 66 : 1. Chicago 2. San Bernardino 3. 1980s (1985) 4. 1920s (1922) 5. Eight 6. Three 7. Kansas with 13 miles 8. The Mother Road 9. It was the first of many McDonald's to spring up along the road 10. Texas 11. Oklahoma with 374.6 miles 12. Amarillo 13. Amarillo 14. Gallup 15. Flagstaff 16. Flagstaff 17. Winona (It rhymes with Arizona) 18. Winona (Also the birthplace of Winona Ryder) 19. Barstow 20. Nat King Cole (Credited to the King Cole Trio the record was a hit in 1946, the year the song was written by Bobby Troup)

SIXTY-SEVEN - POP LYRICS: 1. 'Purple Rain' – Prince 2. 'Your Song' – Elton John 3. 'Empire State of Mind' – Jay Z featuring Alicia Keys (Alicia Keys had a bigger hit with the song but her version does not include this lyric) 4. 'Jolene' – Dolly Parton 5. 'Where the Streets Have No Name' – U2 6. 'Starman' – David Bowie 7. 'Blowin' In the Wind' – Bob Dylan 8. 'Wrecking Ball' – Miley Cyrus 9. 'Wrecking Ball' – Bruce Springsteen 10. 'Dock of the Bay' – Otis Redding 11. 'Roar' – Katy Perry 12. 'I Just Called to Say I Love You' – Stevie Wonder 13. 'Back to Black' – Amy Winehouse 14. 'Poison' – Alice Cooper 15. 'November Rain' – Guns n' Roses 16. 'Brothers In Arms' – Dire Straits 17. 'Crazy' – Gnarls Barkley 18. 'Happy' – Pharrell Williams 19. 'Sympathy For The Devil' – The Rolling Stones 20. 'Steamy Windows' – Tina Turner

SIXTY-EIGHT - GOSSIP COLUMN : 1. Adam Clayton 2. Michael Jackson's 3. Michael Douglas 4. Germany 5. Jennifer Lopez accept J.Lo 6. Henry VIII 7. Demi Moore's 8. Undergoing cosmetic surgery 9. Oxtail 10. Hussein 11. Tom Cruise's 12. Michael Jackson 13. Elvis Presley 14. Kate Winslet 15. Paul McCartney 16. L.B. Johnson 17. Victoria 18. Tony Blair 19. Mike Tyson 20. Bill Clinton

 **ANSWERS**

. . . .

SIXTY-NINE - WORLDWIDE: 1. Washington D.C. 2. Algeria 3. Running of the bulls 4. Yellow 5. Clothes 6. Bahrain 7. Melbourne 8. Japan 9. Las Vegas 10. Netherlands 11. Perth 12. Austria's 13. Miami 14. Africa 15. Japan 16. The Rock of Gibraltar 17. Mexico 18. The Mistral 19. Greece 20. Brazil

SEVENTY - TIMES PAST: 1. Italy 2. Two (Lincoln and Garfield) 3. President Pompidou 4. Japan (This was a reference to the red disc on the Japanese flag) 5. Winston Churchill 6. Philippines 7. Bill Clinton 8. London 9. Russia 10. They used the mix as a contraceptive 11. Korean War 12. His country had no electricity 13. Amin wrote this to Lord Snowdon (Anthony Armstrong-Jones) when he split from Princess Margaret 14. Bathwater 15. Her mother 16. Gerald Ford 17. Nigeria 18. Marble Arch 19. Sicily 20. Five days

SEVENTY-ONE - CALORIE COUNTING : 1. Burger 2. Copper 3. Gouda 4. The pass 5. Munich's 6. Mushroom 7. Nestlé 8. Hellman 9. Wimpy 10. Quince 11. Tangerine 12. Donkey 13. A London club 14. Dipping sauce 15. Vietnam's 16. Shawarma 17. A loaf of bread 18. It is naturally decaffeinated 19. The lava of a moth (People refer to it as a 'worm' which it isn't and the drink is sometimes confused with tequila which it isn't) 20. In a box

SEVENTY-TWO - RANDOM ROCK: 1. Bob Marley 2. Seven 3. 'Money' or 'Time' 4. AC/DC 5. 'The Bodyguard' 6. IV 7. 'Spice' by The Spice Girls 8. 'Born in the USA' 9. The Commodores' 10. 'Into the Groove' 11. 'Where the Streets Have No Name' 12. Prince Charles 13. The Killers' 14. Destiny's Child 15. 'Hounds of Love' 16. Muse 17. Cee Lo Green 18. Elbow 19. Britney Spears 20. Drake

SEVENTY-THREE -NO BUSINESS LIKE SHOW BUSINESS: 1. 'Beauty and the Beast' 2. The Pinball Wizard 3. Cameron Mackintosh 4. 'Aspects of Love' 5. 'West Side Story' 6. Dennis 7. USA 8. Melanie Chisholm (Accept Sporty or Mel C) 9. Carole King 10. 'My Fair Lady' 11. 'The Lion King' 12. Guitar 13. Elizabeth 14. 'Carousel' 15. 'Romeo and Juliet' 16. 'Rent' 17. Seymour 18. Australia 19. 'Singing in the Rain' 20. 'Annie Get Your Gun'

SEVENTY-FOUR - A SPORTING CHANCE: 1. Croquet 2. Boxing 3. Zurich 4. Aachen 5. Wimbledon Women's Singles 6. Beach volleyball 7. Water polo 8. Cricket 9. Ball 10. Badminton 11. Zinedine Zidane 12. Badminton 13. Luge 14. Sumo wrestling 15. He bought it all for himself 16. John McEnroe 17. Venus Williams 18. Five 19. Muhammad Ali 20. Andre Agassi

SEVENTY-FIVE - PAGE BY PAGE: 1. Minas Tirith 2. Moose 3. 'Omoo' 4. The Statue of Liberty 5. Pandaemonium 6. Perry Mason 7. Rabbit 8. 'East of Eden' 9. Four 10. Tinkerbell 11. Forgetfulness 12. 'Captain Courageous' 13. Rat 14. Too-Too 15. Toad 16. 'The Importance of Being Earnest' 17. Twenty years 18. 'The Vampire Chronicles' 19. 'Casino Royale' 20. Children's literature

SEVENTY-SIX - SCENES IN CINEMAS: 1. Nightmare 2. 'Harry Potter and the Goblet of Fire' 3. 'The First Wives Club' 4. Mr Potato Head 5. Humans 6. Parkview Hotel 7. 'Bedknobs and Broomsticks' 8. 'National Lampoon's European Vacation' 9. Ping 10. William Haney 11. James Marshall 12. Pumpkin 13. Rat poisoning 14. Friday 15. Mad Max's 16. Ethel 17. 'Titanic' 18. 'Bridesmaids' 19. 'Top Gun' 20. 'Forrest Gump'

SEVENTY-SEVEN - GERMANY: 1. Beer 2. Muller (In some areas Schmidt is more common but overall Muller is most popular) 3. Daylight saving 4. Oktoberfest 5. Hugo Boss 6. Ulm 7. Berlin 8. Nine 9. 25%. 10. 17th 11. Republic of Korea (South Korea) 12. 80 million (80.2) 13. 29 14. Berlin 15. Second (The Czech Republic is top per capita consumer – not Ireland as listed on some websites) 16. Angela Merkel 17. Ecology 18. Rice Krispies 19. Cologne Cathedral 20. Garden gnomes

SEVENTY-EIGHT - ITALY: 1. Calf (Italia means 'calf land') 2. Michelle Ferrero 3. McDonald's 4. Naples 5. San Marino (The Vatican is only 108 acres) 6. Earthquake 7. The Pantheon 8. Goal 9. Mickey Mouse 10. The evening stroll 11. Violin 12. Switzerland 13. Hope, faith and charity 14. 1990s (1992) 15. 25 (They can vote for the lower house when they are 18) 16. 12th century (1173) 17. Arabs 18. The Trevi Fountain 19. Four 20. Parmigiana Reggiano cheese

. . . .

SEVENTY-NINE - SPAIN: 1. France 2. Gabriel de Castilla 3. El Cid 4. Monkey (The Barbary Macaque, found in Gibraltar, is often called the Barbary Ape but it is a true monkey) 5. Cork 6. Russia 7. Olive oil 8. Cave painting (The painting is a faint red dot thought to be over 40,000 years old) 9. Alhambra 10. Tenerife 11. The Tooth Fairy 12. Penelope Cruz 13. 'Guernica' 14. Tomatoes 15. Madrid 16. Grapes 17. 'Don Quixote' by Miguel Cervantes 18. Bilbao 19. Joan Miro 20. Minorca (Mayo named for the capital Mahon)

EIGHTY - FRANCE: 1. World's tallest bridge (It was structurally the highest and had the highest deck above the ground below) 2. Victor Hugo 3. Salut 4. Crayola 5. Le Dauphin (Dolphin) 6. Denmark 7. Donald Trump 8. Zero 9. Minitel was an early version of the Internet 10. Literature 11. Forging cheques 12. 'Let them eat cake' 13. Jim Morrison's 14. Trousers 15. Pont Neuf (It means New Bridge) 16. Disneyland Paris 17. Green 18. Department store 19. 1970s (1977) 20. Grasse

EIGHTY-ONE - CHINA: 1. Qin Dynasty (Pronounced Chin it is probable that the country was named after this dynasty) 2. Three (Russia, Canada and the U.S.) 3. 20% 4. Toilet paper 5. Crickets 6. One (The whole of China operates to Beijing time) 7. Stamp collecting (philately) 8. Chinese food is chopped small before cooking so knives aren't required 9. First Chinese space walker 10. Beijing 11. The nail on their little finger 12. Decimal weights and measures 13. The Three Gorges Hydroelectric Dam 14. Red 15. Shanghai 16. Carp 17. A single pigtail signifies the woman is married 18. Yangtze (6,300km) 19. Tiananmen Square 20. Table tennis or ping pong (One of the few things China imported from abroad, the game was invented in England.)

EIGHTY-TWO - CANADA: 1. Tides 2. Ten (there are also three territories) 3. Montreal 4. Mount Logan (19,551 feet) 5. Wasaga is the world's longest fresh water beach 6. Three (Baffin, Ellesmere and Victoria) 7. Beauty competitions 8. Loonie (A common loon bird, known as a loonie, is pictured on the coin) 9. Baseball glove 10. 'From sea to sea' 11. Eleven 12. Trivial Pursuit 13. Newfoundland 14. Montreal (Molson Coors Canada is North America's oldest brewery having begun production in 1786) 15. Cheddar 16. Canadian beaver (the largest is the capybara) 17. The C.N. Tower, Toronto 18. Prince Edward Island 19. Six (Toronto, Montreal, Vancouver, Calgary, Edmonton and Ottowa) 20. Six

. . . .

EIGHTY-THREE - RUSSIA: 1. Cats (They keep down the rodents, there were 70 cats at the last count) 2. Street sweeping 3. To prevent pedestrians from being killed by falling icicles 4. Chicken feet 5. In odd numbers (Even numbers of flowers are for funerals) 6. Water 7. Salisbury 8. Fake ambulances 9. The Moskva River 10. Saint Vasily (Accept St Basil as this is what everyone calls him. The cathedral is now a museum) 11. Eleven 12. Judo (Gorbachev recoded a C.D. of romantic ballads) 13. Volga 14. It is the coldest inhabited place on the planet (-67.7C recorded in 1933) 15. They were still using the Julian calendar 16. Beer 17. It is the world's most polluted area of water 18. Pizza 19. Submarines (it was the seventh-largest submarine fleet in the world. 20. They've become addicted to sniffing aviation fuel.

EIGHTY-FOUR - THE SIMPSONS: 1. $847.63 was the estimated amount required to raise a baby for one month 2. Moe (An extra point for his surname Szyslak.) The number is a digit longer than a U.S. phone number and it spells SMITHERS) 3. D'oh 4. Soda (Moe's Bar is edited out of the Arab version) 5. God 6. Comic Book Guy 7. Doh (Not spelt D'oh) 8. Michael Jackson 9. Sideshow Bob 10. 'Ay caramba' 11. Mussolini 12. Cletus (They have 44 children including Crystal Meth, Mary WrestleMania and Normal-Head Joe) 13. Kelsey Grammer (Yes that's how he spells Grammer) 14. That is his school locker combination (Taken from the numbers spoken in AC/DC's 'Dirty Deeds Done Cheap') 15. The French Confection 16. Patty and Selma 17. Paul McCartney 18. 'Excellent' 19. Maude Flanders 20. Apu (Worth at least an extra point if anyone gives his surname which is Nahasapeemapetilon)

EIGHTY-FIVE - ROCK LOCATIONS : 1. Katie Melua 2. Madness 3. The Stranglers 4. Prince 5. The Ramones 6. Siouxsie and the Banshees 7. UB40 8. Bryan Ferry 9. The Four Tops 10. Elvis Costello 11. The Beautiful South 12. Angelic Upstarts 13. Billy Joel 14. Vengaboys 15. Murray Head 16. Boney M 17. The Clash 18. Stevie Wonder 19. Sheryl Crow 20. Chuck Berry

EIGHTY-SIX - MOVIE MAGIC: 1. 'Thunderball' 2. It is extra long 3. Happy 4. 'Surrey With the Fringe on Top' 5. Spanish 6. Skynet 7. Smilex 8. 'The Blues Brothers' 9. SWINGER 10. Rome 11. 'Charlie's Angels: Full Throttle' 12. Alice Cooper 13. Athos 14. 2003 15. Eleven each 16. 'Beverley Hills Cop' 17. Adolf Hitler 18. Cher's ('Alfie' was a U.K. hit for Cilla Black and in the U.S. for Dionne Warwick) 19. 'Apocalypse Now' 20. Bicycle

EIGHTY-SEVEN - CHANNEL HOPPING: 1. The Biscuit 2. Jan Hammer 3. Bud 4. Buck Rogers 5. Coca-Cola 6. Bicycle Repair Man 7. California 8. 'Columbo' 9. From his dead brother's waistcoat (Vest if you're American)10. Al 11. Prince Charles and Diana's wedding 12. Holly 13. Aristotle 14. Galileo 15. He was trying to stop smoking 16. 'CHiPs' (The title based on CHP – California Highway Patrol) 17. Red 18. White 19. One dollar 20. Huckleberry Hound (The island in the Bellinghausen Sea was named Huckleberry Hound by the crew of the Coast Guard Icebreaker U.S. Glacier)

EIGHTY-EIGHT - FUR, FIN AND FEATHER: 1. It's a breed of dog 2. Triangular 3. Avocet 4. Mexico (An axolotl is an amphibian known as the walking fish) 5. Lemur 6. Asia 7. Wild sheep 8. Parrot 9. Scut 10.Tiger 11. Zebra 12. Teeth 13. Ostrich 14. Rhinoceros 15. Black 16. Goose feathers 17. Queen 18. Bloodhound 19. Fox 20. Clowder

EIGHTY-NINE - SCIENTIFIC STUFF: 1. Human cloning 2. Tomato 3. 1970s 4. A new form of bacteria 5. Laudanum 6. Kidney 7. RoboBee 8. Rubber gloves 9. Tornadoes 10. Greenhouse gas emissions 11. India 12. Abu Dhabi 13. Bird flu 14. The Sun 15. Bing 16. Subscriber (Subscriber Identity Module)17. Fish farming 18. Five 19. Mercury 20. Glass

NINETY - THE JACKSONS: 1. Andrew Jackson 2. Peter Jackson 3. Janet Jackson 4. Mahalia Jackson 5. Paris (She is Paris Michael Katherine Jackson) 6. Jackson Pollock 7. Samuel L. Jackson 8. Jackie Jackson 9. Tito Jackson 10. Jesse Jackson 11. Stonewall 12. Wanda Jackson 13. Glenda Jackson 14. La Toya Jackson 15. Jackson Brown 16. Colin Jackson 17. 'Stargate' 18. P.G. Wodehouse 19. Gordon Jackson 20. Katherine (She was born Kattie. B Screws but insisted on being known as Katherine Esther Jackson)

NINETY-ONE - 2015: 1. That's the number of people killed by U.S. cops in the year 2. 'Star Wars – The Force Awakens' 3. Gwyneth Paltrow 4. IKEA catalogue Approximately 210 million copies, 62 versions distributed in 43 countries in 30 languages, by comparison approximately 100 million Bibles were published) 5. Caitlyn, formerly Bruce, had undergone sex reassignment surgery 6. Guantanamo Bay 7. Japan 8. Charlie Hebdo 9. They were on stage when terrorists attacked the Paris Bataclan concert hall 10. Nigeria 11. Germanwings 12. Singapore 13. Tunis 14. Pam 15. Baltimore 16. Ireland 17. Cuba 18. Singapore 19. Hajj 20. China allowed parents to have a second child

. . . .

NINETY-TWO - GEOGRAPHICAL: 1. Jamaica 2. El Salvador 3. Wells 4. English 5. Seville 6. Dubrovnik 7. Paris, Charles de Gaulle 8. Danish 9. Botswana 10. Stuttgart 11. Niagara 12. Antwerp 13. Cave 14. Riviera 15. Greece 16. Windsor (Not to each other!) 17. Volcano 18. High Street 19. The Giant's Causeway 20. The Arabian Peninsula

NINETY-THREE - BEEN AND GONE: 1. The Duke of Wellington 2. Saxophone 3. Tobacco 4. Saddam Hussein 5. Poland 6. Ronald Reagan with Nancy 7. Golf 8. They both used the same toothpaste (Colgate) 9. Theodore Roosevelt 10. Archbishop Desmond Tutu 11. Princess Anne the Princess Royal 12. They were hurricanes 13. Pope John Paul II 14. Fifteen years 15. Private (He was given the honorary title Kentucky Colonel) 16. John Major 17. France 18. Suez Canal 19. Ethiopia 20. Seven

NINETY-FOUR - LIQUID REFRESHMENT: 1. September (Although named the Oktoberfest it always begins in September) 2. Green 3. Harvey Wallbanger 4. Absinthe 5. Tea (Usually green tea) 6. Vodka 7. Pepsi-Cola 8. Bushmills 9. Welsh 10. Plymouth 11. Cognac 12. Champagne or sparkling white wine (A standard Kir is white wine with a dash of Crème de Cassis) 13. Tequila 14. Coffee beans (A single coffee bean in Sambuca is known as 'con la mosca' or 'the fly' but strictly speaking there should be three beans representing health, happiness and prosperity) 15. Blackcurrant 16. Benedictine 17. November 18. Retsina 19. Port 20. It is the scientific name for the fear of being faced with an empty beer glass

NINETY-FIVE - THINGS TO WEAR: 1.Prada 2. Miami 3. T-shirt 4. Kate Moss 5. John Galliano 6. Size labels 7. Shoes 8. Muffin top 9. Milan 10. Karl Lagerfeld 11. Miss Sixty 12. Quicksilver 13. Vivienne Westwood 14. Manufacturer's labels 15. Victoria Beckham (Posh) 16. Australia 17. Mini skirt 18. Rah-rah skirt 19. Versace 20. Thomas Burberry

NINETY-SIX - EXOTIC MENU: 1. Yoghurt 2. The Fat Duck 3. Hotest chilli 4. Turmeric 5. Sashimi (Sushi means 'sour tasting' and is made from soured rice, it does not have to contain raw fish) 6. Buffalo 7. Guinea pig 8. It is a type of snail 9. Fat (Usually the duck's own fat) 10. Plank (This refers to its shape when sliced) 11. Dog meat (Cat meat is called Thit meo) 12. Horse 13. Tripe 14. Saliva (Their nests are stuck together with saliva that is soaked out to flavour the soup) 15. Liver 16. Mushrooms 17. Cock's comb 18. Golden 19. Tapioca 20. Coriander

. . . .

NINETY-SEVEN - AMERICAN ROCK STARS: 1. Red Hot Chili Peppers 2. 'Telephone' 3. Robin Thicke 4. Nile Rodgers 5. Lady Gaga 6. 'Heartbreak Hotel' 7. Lou Reed 8. Bob Dylan 9. Cheap Trick 10. Kim Basinger 11. Eddie Van Halen 12. 'In Dreams' 13. The Jacksons' 14. Lionel Richie 15. Cher 16. 'Girls Just Want to Have Fun' 17. 'Like a Prayer' 18. 'Get on the bus' 19. The Osmonds 20. 'Citizen Kane'

NINETY-EIGHT - MORE MUSICALS: 1. Elsa (Full name Baroness Elsa Schraeder) 2. 'Kiss Me Kate' 3. 'Oklahoma' 4. 'They Call the Wind Maria' 5. His slippers 6. London 7. Horse racing 8. 'The King and I' 9. 'People' 10. 'Send In The Clowns' 11. 'Good Morning Starshine' 12. 'The Wiz' 13. 'Evita' 14. 'Spamalot' 15. Jane and Michael 16. 'Aladdin' 17. 'Kinky Boots' 18. Dillmount 19. Diana Ross 20. She was pregnant

NINETY-NINE - BALLS: 1. Royal Troon (It's a tiny green and the shortest hole in championship golf) 2. Number Eight 3. American Express 4. Jones 5. Boris Becker 6. Boules 7. Real Madrid 8. Bowls 9. Australian Rules Football (Often known just as Australian Rules) 10. Lacrosse 11. Pete Sampras 12. Skip 13. Throw-off 14. U.S.A. 15. Maria Sharapova 16. Paris Saint-Germain 17. Real tennis 18. White 19. Let 20. Seven

ONE HUNDRED - THE SUMMER GAMES: 1. Paris 2. Marathon 3. Wrestling 4. Afghanistan 5. Many were cremated as they settled on the bowl where the Olympic flame was ignited 6. Bjork 7. Venus Williams 8. Drug tests 9. Sydney 10. He was officially a spectator 11. China 12. 1,500 metres 13. Lennox Lewis 14. An Olympic medal 15. Backstroke 16. Cuba 17. France was the only team to enter 18. Great Britain 19. A urine sample (She submitted someone else's urine instead of her own) 20. 400 metres

ONE HUNDRED AND ONE - WRITERS: 1. Friday 2. 'As You Like It' 3. 'Great Expectations' 4. P.D. James 5. Ian Fleming 6. 'Popcorn' 7. Harold Pinter 8. The weather 9. 'The Moonstone' 10. H.G. Wells 11. 'Rebecca' 12. 'Eyes Wide Shut' 13. Bob Dylan 14. Romeo 15. 'Fahrenheit 451' 16. 'Drink it himself' 17. Ruth Rendell 18. Haggis 19. Oyster 20. Georges Simenon (Creator of Maigret)

ANSWERS

ONE HUNDRED AND TWO - IN THE PLOT: 1. Abel 2. Walter Mitty 3. Fifteen 4. U2 (A chapter is set during the 'Joshua Tree' tour) 5. Toasted cheese 6. Fourth (She says she is in her thirty-second year of being single) 7. Strider 8. A rhinoceros 9. Edinburgh 10. Hazel 11. Donkey 12. Garlic 13. Bump 14. 42 15. Four (Frodo Baggins, Samwise Gamgee, Peregrin Took and Meriadoc Brandybuck) 16. The Prancing Pony 17. 'The Satanic Verses' 18. Miss Lemon 19. Spider-Man 20. Ten-years

ONE HUNDRED AND THREE - PAINTERS AND PAINTINGS: 1. Henri 2. 'The Scream' 3. Leonardo da Vinci 4. Paul Gaugin 5. Florence (It hangs in the Uffizi) 6. Bass 7. Amsterdam 8. Barcelona's 9. Bono 10. Velasquez 11. Rijksmuseum, Amsterdam 12. Chairman Mao Zedong 13. Salvador Dali's 14. Spanish 15. Johannes Vermeer 16. Green 17. David Hockney's 18. Roy Lichtenstein 19. 'The Laughing Cavalier' by Frans Hals 20. Jeff Koons

ONE HUNDRED AND FOUR - THE MOVING IMAGE: 1. Surfing 2. 'Gone With the Wind' 3. 'The Impossible' 4. 'Spider-Man' 5. Nicole Kidman 6. 'Jurassic Park' 7. 'Full Metal Jacket' 8. Pamela Anderson 9. Cher 10. 'Monty Python and the Holy Grail' 11. Bob Dylan 12. Mashed potato 13. 'Over the Rainbow' 14. Soap 15. Partial sight 16. 'Frozen' 17. A candle 18. Frank Sinatra 19. Wallace and Gromit 20. 'King Kong'

ONE HUNDRED AND FIVE - PEAK TIME TV: 1. 'SpongeBob SquarePants' 2. Laramie 3. Osama bin Laden 4. Ant and Dec 5. She had a baby (The main controversy over the incident was that she smoked during her pregnancy) 6. Mode 7. 'The Office' 8. Rebecca Howe 9. Pam Dawber 10. Daisy Duke 11. 'Melrose Place' 12. Doctor (Dr Nick obtained his medical degree from the Hollywood Upstairs Medical College) 13. Kirstin Shepherd 14. Jessica Fletcher 15. Gerald Ford 16. Tanner 17. Alligator (Elvis lived on a boat with James 'Sonny' Crockett) 18. Galvatron 19. Thomas Cromwell 20. 'Power Rangers'

ONE HUNDRED AND SIX - CALL THE DOCTOR: 1. Nitrogen 2. Bark 3. Kidney 4. Tokyo 5. German measles 6. Malaria 7. In front of the ear 8. Twelve 9. Bile 10. Tears 11. In the eyes 12. Ligament 13. Foetus 14. Five 15. The wrist 16. A stroke 17. Liver 18. Tendon 19. Abdomen 20. The first stage

• •

ONE HUNDRED AND SEVEN - ANIMALS: 1. Cheetah 2. Duck-billed platypus 3. Wombat 4. Size of ears (African elephants have larger ears to fan themselves in extreme heat) 5. Goat milk 6. Two 7. Seven 8. Giraffe 9. Pheasant 10. They were to supply hot water for elephant showers 11. Rat 12. Seals 13. Antelope 14. Two 15. Koala 16. Madagascar 17. Tyrannosaurus Rex 18. Afrikaans 19. Tigers 20. Three-toed sloth

ONE HUNDRED AND EIGHT - TECHNOLOGY: 1. Fountain pens 2. The Sinclair C5 (Battery and pedal-powered car) 3. Volvo 4. Charger cables 5. Turin 6. Cell phones 7. A King of Denmark and Norway (Harold Bluetooth ruled between about 940 and 986) 8. 2001 9. Birmingham Small Arms (Originally manufacturers of military and sporting firearms) 10. It was in the form of a clothing clip 11. Malaysia's 12. Optics 13. Red and white 14. Airbus A380 15. Blackberry 16. Mercedes-Benz 17. Eight-track 18. Skateboards 19. The Eiffel Tower 20. To carry spare batteries

ONE HUNDRED AND NINE - FOLK WHO FOUND FAME: 1. Amy Winehouse 2. Vegetarian 3.Paris Hilton 4. Sting 5. Diana Ross 6. Bono 7. Her heart 8. Rennée Zellweger 9. John Lennon 10. Richard Burton 11. Speak 12. Kate Moss 13. Gladys 14. Alcohol rehab clinic 15. The summit of Everest 16. Italian 17. Lhasa 18. Britney Spears 19. Barbra Streisand 20. She's his mother

ONE HUNDRED AND TEN - IT'S A MAD WORLD: 1. Nothing 2. February 14th   St Valentine's Day 3. Santa Claus (Bells Nichols fills empty plates with cake and cookies on New Year's Eve) 4. Jimmy Carter 5. Woodpeckers 6. KFC 7. Apricots (There was an unexplained belief that apricots led to tanks breaking down during World War II) 8. Eat a meal 9. Blood donor 10. Netherlands' 11. A cup of tea   12. Vegetables (Other than potatoes) 13. Virginia 14. Everything 15. Jonathan Edwards was Roosevelt's pet bear 16. Monkeys 17. Cheese 18. Internet access 19. It was demolished and the wood used to build a barn 20. Japan

ONE HUNDRED AND ELEVEN - 1980s: 1. Yuri Andropov 2. David Linley 3. To find an acting job 4. A Kit Kat chocolate bar 5. Beer flavour 6. Boot-shaped 7. Brighton 8. Leeds United 9. Garbage Pail Kids 10. 'All Creatures Great and Small' 11. Snow 12. IRA spokespersons (They still got their messages out but their voices were dubbed by actors) 13. Moshe Dayan 14. Roy Orbison 15. Andy Capp 16. Arthur Negus 17. Thomas Hearns 18. Their council houses 19. Jobs 20. Jersey

. . . .

ONE HUNDRED AND TWELVE - MORE 1980s: 1. Nineteen 2. The Green Goddess 3. Once (1986) 4. White 5. Steve Interesting Davis 6. Gob-smacked 7. The Roly Polys 8. Their kidneys 9. The State Pension 10. Dennis Wilson (Both died in 1983) 11. 'Eloise' 12. Mathias Rust 13. Enniskillen 14. Ballroom dancing 15. Sandy Lyle 16. 'Bullseye' 17. Cynthia Payne 18. Cornetto 19. Uncle Albert 20. 'OTT'

ONE HUNDRED AND THIRTEEN - 1990s: 1. Sarah Kennedy 2. Swampy 3. Melinda Messenger 4. Eternal 5. Three 6. Martin Bell 7. Queen Elizabeth II 8. 'The Hunchback of Notre Dame' 9. On the tailfin of British Airways' planes 10. Eric Cantona 11. Formula One 12. Princess Diana's funeral 13. Martina Hingis 14. Jupiter 15. Gloucester 16. Sumo wrestling 17. Barbara Cartland 18. Dame Shirley Porter 19. Wonderbra 20. Faulty breast implants

ONE HUNDRED AND FOURTEEN - MORE 1990s: 1. Rear of the Year 2. The Black Dyke Band 3. The Spice Girls 4. Ben and Jerry's ice cream 5. They were saving the country money 6. VAT was added 7. 'Some Might Say' 8. Apart 9. 'Four Weddings and a Funeral' 10. Bill Wyman 11. Polly Pocket toys 12. Advertise 13. Land and/or property 14. It was his 'Spitting Image' puppet 15. Wheel clamping on private land 16. On £10 notes 17. Michaelangelo (The misspelling was later corrected to Michelangelo) 18. 'God Save the Queen 19. Strawberries and cream 20. Karaoke

ONE HUNDRED AND FIFTEEN - BOARD GAMES: 1. Three 2. Bishop 3. Kylie Minogue 4. Six 5. Ten 6. Five 7. 15 8. By throwing a six 9. Kingdoms 10. Monopoly 11. Canada 12. Chess 13. GO 14. Krusty the Clown 15. Ten 16. Two 17. Six 18. Red 19. Four 20. Souvenirs

ONE HUNDRED AND SIXTEEN - GREAT FOR GOURMETS: 1. Grilling 2. Mayonnaise 3. Consommé Royale 4. Red cabbage 5. Suffolk 6. Lobster 7. Wasabi 8. In citrus juice 9. Vinegar 10. A poached egg 11. A skillet 12. Ham (Accept pork) 13. Rum 14. Garlic 15. Drambuie 16. Cheek 17. Cheese (Being Welsh the sausage also includes leek) 18. Chicken tikka masala 19. Portugal 20. Three

ONE HUNDRED AND SEVENTEEN - MORE TASTY TREATS: 1. Guard of Honour 2. Kick is the correct name for the concave bottom of a bottle 3. Two-one 4. Brawn 5. Leek 6. Salamander 7. Pepper mill 8. The Isle of Skye 9. Octopus 10. Keith Floyd 11. Bombay mix 12. Lemon

juice 13. White or green grapes 14. Salted peanuts 15. Grolsch 16. Choux pastry 17. Seaweed 18. Kiss 19. Hollandaise 20. A sandwich (It's the number of slices of bread)

ONE HUNDRED AND EIGHTEEN - THAT'S ENTERTAINMENT: 1. Annie Lennox 2. Rider 3. 22nd 4. Major Gowan 5. 'Monty Python's Flying Circus' 6. Blondie's 7. Five 8. REM 9. 'A View to a Kill' 10. Drink alcohol 11. Cars 12. 'Groundhog Day' 13. Radiohead 14. Only female dinosaurs were created 15. 'Hamlet' 16. Mick Jagger 17. Placido Domingo 18. Cirque du Soleil 19. The second E 20. Gladioli

ONE HUNDRED AND NINETEEN - JET SETTING: 1. Libya 2. Rome 3. U.S. Dollar 4. Jamaica 5. Four 6. Canada's 7. Sugared almonds 8. Sleeping Beauty's 9. Cairo 10. Tupelo 11. Melbourne, Australia 12. Bahamas 13. Havana 14. Bristol's 15. Key Largo 16. Corfu 17. Goat 18. Lesbosians 19. Venice 20. Newark

ONE HUNDRED AND TWENTY - YESTERDAYS: 1. The Alamo 2. Bee 3. Wilson 4. Switzerland 5. Pope John Paul II's funeral 6. Saddam Hussein 7. Ian Paisley 8. Smoking 9. Paris 10. Mother Teresa 11. Their religion forecast the end of the world prior to the Summer (They later changed the date to 2012) 12. Ronald Reagan 13. Egypt 14. Breathalyzer tests 15. Scrap dealers 16. Slavery 17. Indira Gandhi 18. Guardian Angels 19. Winnie Mandela's Football Club 20. Rhodesia

ONE HUNDRED AND TWENTY-ONE - FEMALE FASHIONS: 1. Spray tans 2. Gucci 3. Gisele Bundchen 4. Roberto Cavalli 5. Adidas 6. Shoulder pads 7. 'Flashdance' 8. Leg warmers 9. A scrunchie 10. Nicole Richie 11. Glow 12. Jennifer Aniston 13. Hilary Swank 14. Ballet shoes 15. Agent Provocateur 16. Drew Barrymore 17. Nail polish 18. Five 19. Yves St Laurent 20. Sapphire

ONE HUNDRED AND TWENTY-TWO - HEY ROCK AND ROLL: 1. Beard (Frank Beard) 2. 'Billy Jean' 3. 'Careless Whisper' 4. Pierrot (Accept Clown) 5. Friday (The opening words are: 'Friday night and the lights are low') 6. The Revolution 7. Del Shannon 8. 'Parachutes' 9. 'The Beatles' 10. 27 11. The Faces 12. Electric Light Orchestra (accept ELO) 13. '1984' is the title and also the year of release 14. Margaret Thatcher 15. Three Dog Night 16. Blind Faith 17. Aerosmith 18. 'Johnny B. Goode' 19. Shoes 20. The Kinks

• •

ONE HUNDRED AND TWENTY-THREE - COMPOSERS: 1. Richard Strauss 2. Ninth 3. 'Alien' 4. Nagasaki 5. Warsaw 6. Egypt 7. Mozart 8. Egypt 9. Beethoven 10. 'The Messiah' 11. 'Lohengrin' 12. Mozart 13. Richard Wagner's 14. Schubert's 15. It's the Nokia ringtone 16. Benjamin Britten 17. 'The Marriage of Figaro' 18. 1914 19. Joseph Haydn's (After his funeral in 1809 two men bribed the gravedigger to allow them to sever and steal the head. It passed from hand to hand until being reunited with the body in 1932. A replacement skull had been added to the skeleton so Haydn is now buried with two skulls) 20. 'The New World Symphony' (The 'Going Home' section is best known from the Hovis commercial with the boy and his bike on a steep hill)

ONE HUNDRED AND TWENTY-FOUR - YOU HAVE TO BE FIT: 1. Japan's 2. Blue 3. The Wall 4. Big Daddy 5. Indoor records 6. Clothing 7. Michael Jordan 8. Take-over zone 9. Joe Frazier 10. The previous winner 11. A basket 12. Austria 13. Gymnasium 14. Three 15. Dog mushing 16. Zorbing 17. Elephant polo 18. Huddersfield Town 19. Water 20. Epsom

ONE HUNDRED AND TWENTY-FIVE - FIVE RINGS: 1. Norway with 39, followed by Germany 31 and Canada 29 2. Munich's 3. Weymouth 4. All the competitors were black 5. A corner of the Olympic flag 6. Rings 7. Three (Discus, shot and javelin) 8. Bullfight posters 9. Andy Murray 10. Taekwondo 11. Athens 12. Strawberry 13. Eight 14. Canada boycotted the Games 15. CCCP 16. Rio de Janeiro 17. Defect (She defected at the 1948 London Games while coaching the gold medal-winning Czech ladies gymnastic team) 18. U.S.A. 19. Curling 20. Seoul

ONE HUNDRED AND TWENTY-SIX - FICTIONAL CHARACTERS: 1. Endeavour 2. Beer drinking 3. Father Brown 4. June 5. 'Brighton Rock' 6. Claire 7. Water vole 8. Fox 9. Kala 10. Porthos 11. Woodhouse 12. Jay 13. Tom 14. Manslaughter 15. Magnus Pym 16. Darling 17. Sir Samuel Vine 18. Edmund 19. 'Les Miserables' 20. James Bond

ONE HUNDRED AND TWENTY-SEVEN - INDIA: 1. Zero (and no rupees can be brought out) 2. Banana 3. The Taj Mahal 4. Coloured powder (and water) 5. Chess (The word means 'four members of an army') 6. Saffron 7. They depict explicit sexual activities 8. Cotton 9. Suttee 10. Himalaya 11. His ears 12. Jaipur 13. 1947 (It began in 1858) 14. Hinduism 15. Bombay 16. Mahatma 17. Mango 18. Indian railways 19. One (India Standard Time) 20. Six (In addition to the usual four India has Summer Monsoon and Winter Monsoon)

• •

ONE HUNDRED AND TWENTY-EIGHT - NATIONAL DISHES:
1. Mutton or lamb 2. Couscous 3. Moules-frites (Mussels with potato fries) 4. Rice 5. Cuba 6. Denmark's 7. Succotash 8. Conch 9. Béchamel 10. Paprika 11. Lentils 12. Fried egg 13. Mutton or lamb 14. Seaweed 15. Coconut cream 16. Chicken 17. Sausage 18. New Zealand 19. Cabbage 20. Rosti

ONE HUNDRED AND TWENTY-NINE - BEATLES LYRICS: 1. 'Roll Over Beethoven' 2. 'All My Loving' 3. 'Do You Want to Know a Secret?' 4. 'I Should Have Known Better' 5. 'Eleanor Rigby' 6. 'Baby You're a Rich Man' 7. 'Hello, Goodbye' 8. 'Revolution' 9. 'Free As A Bird' 10. 'Let It Be' 11. 'Come Together' 12. 'The Ballad of John and Yoko' 13. 'Rain' 14. 'Day Tripper' 15. 'I Feel Fine' 16. 'Things We Said Today' 17. 'Ain't She Sweet' 18. 'I'm Down' 19. 'Yellow Submarine' 20. 'Lady Madonna'

ONE HUNDRED AND THIRTY - STONES SINGLES: 1. 'Jumpin' Jack Flash' 2. 'Little Red Rooster' 3. 'Play With Fire' 4. 'The Last Time' 5. 'It's All Over Now' 6. 'Not Fade Away' 7. 'Get Off Of My Cloud' 8. 'Paint 'It Black' 9. 'Ruby Tuesday' 10. 'Time Is On My Side' 11. 'Lady Jane' 12. '(I Can't Get No) Satisfaction' 13. 'She's a Rainbow' 14. 'As Tears Go By' 15. 'Sympathy for the Devil' 16. 'Brown Sugar' 17. 'Fool to Cry' 18. 'Streets of Love' 19. 'Wild Horses' 20. 'Doom and Gloom'

ONE HUNDRED AND THIRTY-ONE - ROCK DIVA LYRICS: 1. '(Flashdance) What a Feelin'' 2. 'One More Time' 3. 'Crazy in Love' 4. 'No More Drama' 5. 'Jupiter' 6. 'Spinning Around' 7. 'Firework' 8. 'Gloria' 9. 'Honey' 10. 'Here I Am' 11. 'Ain't Got No-I Got Life' 12. 'Rehab' 13. 'What's Love Got To Do With It?' 14. 'A Natural Woman' 15. 'Piece Of My Heart' 16. 'Woodstock' 17. 'People Have the Power' 18. 'Love Has No Pride' 19. 'Sweet Dreams' 20. 'Midnight Train to Georgia'

ONE HUNDRED AND THIRTY-TWO - NATIONAL SPORTS: 1. Buzkashi 2. Pato 3. Yacht racing 4. Kabaddi 5. Cricket 6. Archery 7. Lacrosse 8. Ice hockey (Known simply as 'hockey' in Canada) 9. Chilean Rodeo 10. Table tennis 11. Baseball 12. Rugby Union 13. Sumo Wrestling 14. Basketball 15. Rugby Union 16. Cross-country skiing 17. Taekwondo 18. Alpine skiing 19. Field hockey 20. Volleyball

● ●

ONE HUNDRED AND THIRTY-THREE - OSCARS BEST ACTOR:
1. 'The African Queen' 2. Marlon Brando 3. 'The Revenant' 4. Stephen Hawking ('The Theory of Everything') 5. Jean Dujardin (2011 'The Artist') 6. Colin Frith 7. Adrien Brody 8. 'Training Day' 9. Nicholas Cage 10. Tom Hanks (For 'Philadelphia' and 'Forrest Gump) 11. 'Scent of a Woman' 12. Daniel Day-Lewis ('My Left Foot,' 'There Will Be Blood' and 'Lincoln') 13. Jake LaMotta ('Raging Bull') 14. Two ('Kramer vs Kramer' and 'Rain Man') 15. 'Milk' 16. Idi Amin 17. Ray Charles ('Ray') 18. Lester Burnham 19. Gordon Gekko 20. 'As Good as it Gets'

ONE HUNDRED AND THIRTY-FOUR - OSCARS BEST ACTRESS:
1. Ingrid Bergman 2. 'Roman Holiday' 3. Jane Fonda 4. Two ('Sophie's Choice' and 'The Iron Lady') 5. Jessica Tandy ('Driving Miss Daisy') 6. 'Blue Sky' 7. Halle Berry ('Monster's Ball') 8. June Carter Cash 9. Marion Cotillard (Edith Piaf in 'La Vie en Rose') 10. Marlee Matlin (She was 21 and for the same movie also became the first deaf actress to win) 11. Howland 12. Cate Blanchett 13. Sandra Bullock ('The Blind Side') 14. Nicole Kidman 15. 'Boys Don't Cry' 16. 'Shakespeare In Love' 17. Kathy Bates 18. 'The Accused' 19. 'Mary Poppins' 20. 'A Streetcar Named Desire'

ONE HUNDRED AND THIRTY-FIVE - ROCK AND ROLL HALL OF FAME : 1.Cleveland 2. Lake Erie 3. Yoko Ono (Mrs John Lennon) 4. The Rolling Stones 5. New York (At the Waldorf Astoria Hotel) 6. They were originally left out when their lead singers, Buddy Holly and Bill Haley, were inducted as solo artists 7. The Everly Brothers (In the first year 1986) 8. 25 years 9. Charlotte Church 10. Electric Light Orchestra (ELO) 11. Bill Withers 12. Ringo Starr 13. The Paul Butterfield Blues Band 14. 50% 15. The Teenagers (They were nominated eight times prior to induction in 1993) 16. The Supremes 17. The Yardbirds 18. Duane Eddy 19. Solomon Burke 20. Dusty Springfield

ONE HUNDRED AND THIRTY-SIX - WHO SAID WHAT?: 1. Winston Churchill 2. Germaine Greer 3. Virginia Woolf 4. William Shakespeare (From 'Henry VIII') 5. King George V 6. Nancy Mitford 7. Oscar Wilde 8. P.G. Wodehouse 9. Brendan Behan 10. Sir John Betjeman 11. Margaret Thatcher 12. Bob Dylan 13. Martin Luther King Jr 14. John Lennon 15. Abraham Lincoln 16. Adolf Hitler 17. Cole Porter 18. Paul Simon 19. Timothy Leary 20. David Frost

ANSWERS

. . . .

ONE HUNDRED AND THIRTY-SEVEN - YOUNG LITERATURE: 1. Harry Potter and the Order of the Phoenix' 2. Humpty Dumpty 3. Brer Rabbit 4. Tom Sawyer 5. 'Toad of Toad Hall' 6. James (He isn't named in the book but in the movie Santa gives him a present and the label says 'James') 7. Mr McGregor's 8. A monkey 9. Max 10. The Gruffalo 11. Christmas Eve 12. 60th 13. 'Snow White' 14. 'The Secret Garden' 15. Sophie (Based on Dahl's granddaughter, model and actress Sophie Dahl)16. 'Five Children and It' 17. Winnie the Pooh's 18. Swedish 19. Shirley 20. 'Witches'

ONE HUNDRED AND THIRTY-EIGHT - FRAME IT: 1. A nude 2. Marilyn Monroe 3. David Hockney 4. Gin Lane 5. Elephant dung 6. Horses 7. Sarah Lucas 8. 'The Blue Boy' 9. The Pre-Raphaelite Brotherhood 10. Edwin Landseer's 11. J.M.W. Turner's 12. Walter Raleigh's 13. David Hockney 14. Blue 15. Winston Churchill's 16. 1920s 17. Max Ernst 18. Pointilism 19. Gustav Klimt's 20. Henri Matisse's

ONE HUNDRED AND THIRTY-NINE - BIG AT THE BOX OFFICE: 1. 'Brokeback Mountain' 2. 'Philadelphia' 3. 'Fatal Attraction' 4. The Blues Brothers 5. 'Wall Street' 6. Beyonce Knowles 7. Shawshank 8. 'La La Land' 9. Pigs 10. 'Cool Hand Luke' 11. '8 Mile' 12. Tokyo 13. 'Goodfellas' 14. Nicolle Kidman 15. 'Rosebud' 16. Baltimore 17. Boo 18. 'Not practise it.' 19. 'American Pie' 20. Baseball

ONE HUNDRED AND FORTY - REMOTE CONTROL: 1. Women 2. Atlanta 3. Emma Thompson 4. 'South Park' 5. The Alabama 3 6. Ten 7. Twice 8. 'Star Trek' 9. Shaggy 10. Orson 11. Television 12. 'The Flintstones' 13. Gary 14. Seven 15. Basset Hound 16. Ross 17. Rhode Island 18. 'Gossip Girl' 19. Insurance 20. Scott McCall

ONE HUNDRED AND FORTY-ONE - MORE BODY BITS: 1. Vitamin K 2. Muscles 3. Vitamin D 4. Collar bone 5. Elbow 6. The brain 7. Nostrils 8. Phobia 9. Behind the navel 10. Two 11. Greenstick 12. Hands on knees 13. Veins 14. Pupils 15. Wrist 16. Pregnant 17. Tongue studs 18. Finger length 19. Walk 20. His buttocks

. . . .

ONE HUNDRED AND FORTY-TWO - ERNIE THE MILKMAN: 1. Market Street 2. His badge 3. Sue 4. Linley Lane, number twenty-two 5. Haughty, proud and chic 6. His cocoa 7. Bathe in milk 8. Pasteurised 9. That tickled old Ernie 10. Two Ton Ted from Teddington 11. Treacle tarts 12. Hot meat pies 13. A macaroon 14. Hot rolls 15. Crumpets 16. Half past four 17. His gold top 18. Strawberry 19. A rock cake 20. A stale pork pie

ONE HUNDRED AND FORTY-THREE - PLANTS AND TREES: 1. Avocado 2. White 3. Bonsai tree 4. Trees 5. Cranberry 6. Flax 7. Oak 8. Pear 9. Oregano 10. Jasmine 11. Palm oil 12. Grapefruit 13. Christmas tree 14. It produces the world's largest fruit 15. A herb is from the leaf, a spice from any other part of the plant 16. Hops 17. Passion fruit 18. It was hit by a drunk driver (The tree in Niger on the edge of the Sahara was 250 miles from any other living tree) 19. It won't, marks on bark stay at the same height 20. It is the world's largest flower (About ten feet high and three feet wide and very smelly)

ONE HUNDRED AND FORTY-FOUR - DOMESTIC SCIENCE: 1. Glue 2. Artificial Christmas tree 3. Automatic turn-off 4. Can opener 5. Frozen chicken 6. Wine box 7. Toothpaste tube 8. Sweden 9. Pyrex 10. Bra strap 11. Cigarettes 12. Teflon 13. TV remote control 14. Telephone answering machine 15. Grated cheese 16. Linoleum 17. Lactic acid 18. Soda water 19. Jacuzzi 20. iPhone

ONE HUNDRED AND FORTY-FIVE - CELEBRITY SCANDALS: 1. Bruce Willis 2. Keifer Sutherland 3. Tom Cruise 4. Jim Threapleton 5. Hugh Grant 6. Jennifer Aniston 7. Madonna 8. Johnny Depp 9. Melanie Griffith 10. Nicholas Cage 11. J.K. Rowling 12. It became 'Wino Forever' 13. Woody Allen 14. Burger King 15. Madonna 16. Burt Reynolds 17. Elizabeth Taylor 18. Two 19. Princess Diana 20. George Michael's

ONE HUNDRED AND FORTY-SIX - MISCELLANEOUS: 1. On submarines 2. Spam 3. Doom Bar (Owned by Molson Coors) 4. Sixteen (with an average of 800 kernels per cob) 5. Colombia 6. It was assassinated (The dog put his muddy paws on a drunk in the street and the man stabbed it to death) 7. Jack 8. The zoo's elephant 9. The order of Prince Charles' names (Charles Philip Arthur George) 10. Stevie Wonder 11. Uniform 12. Earrings 13. Seven 14. Fifteen 15. Cleaning perspiration from clothes 16. Ashtrays 17. Sauna 18. Nazareth 19. A stripper 20. Feeding pigeons

ONE HUNDRED AND FORTY-SEVEN - PLACES: 1. Yellowstone 2. Colorado 3. The Eiffel Tower 4. The Golden Gate Bridge 5. Petra 6. River Nile 7. France 8. Coconuts 9. Peru 10. Morocco 11. Sri Lanka 12. Singapore 13. Stuttgart 14. The North Pole 15. Brixton 16. Capri 17. Athens 18. Tunisia 19. Tonga 20. Seven

ONE HUNDRED AND FORTY-EIGHT - COMEDY SONGS: 1. 'They're Coming to Take Me Away, Ha Haaa' (The b-side is the same song played backwards) 2. Sunscreen 3. Sophia Loren 4. 'Jingle Bells' 5. Roller skate 6. 'Shaddap You Face' by the Joe Dolce Music Theatre 7. 'Monster Mash' 8. Charley Brown 9. 'Rabbit' 10. A dustman 11. A Moron 12. 'Disco Duck' 13. 'Itsy Bitsy Teenie Weenie Yellow Polka Dot Bikini' 14. 'Leader of the Laundromat' 15. Tiny Tim's 16. 'My Ding-a-Ling' 17. A dead skunk 18. A deckchair 19. Alexei Sayle 20. George Formby's (The BBC played his 'With My Little Stick of Blackpool Rock' which is even more suggestive)

ONE HUNDRED AND FORTY-NINE - PASSING FADS: 1. Second watch 2. Madonna 3. Lemon 4. The Aldi-effect 5. Alexander McQueen's 6. Bomber jackets 7. Unibrow 8. Black 9. Cabbage Patch Kids 10. The Beastie Boys 11. Preenies 12. M.C. Hammer 13. Break-dancing 14. February 14th, St Valentine's Day 15. Collars 16. The Macarena 17. Nehru 18. 1922 19. Bell-bottoms 20. Care Bears

ONE HUNDRED AND FIFTY - THE FINAL COUNTDOWN: 1. Burning at the stake (She was convicted of coining – cutting metal from coins to make more coins) 2. Bonaparte 3. Lord Louis Mountbatten 4. Cleopatra 5. George I (His native and only language was German) 6. Miss Canada 7. Dodo 8. 'Bridge Over Troubled Waters' 9. Marilyn Monroe (From the 1961 movie 'The Misfits') 10. This is the last year they were all included in the Olympics (Paris) 11. 1944 12. 2003 13. Nine 14. Eugene Cernan 15. 'King Kong' 16. Bon Jovi 17. Dopey 18. W.C. Fields (Carlotta was his long-time mistress) 19. Larry Fortensky 20. Clarksville

The Quizmaster's QUIZ BOOK

Index

1. Human Nature
2. Lifestyle
3. History
4. Pop and Rock Oldies
5. Sports
6. Classical Music and Musicals
7. Olympics
8. The Written Word
9. Art and Artists
10. Movies
11. TV
12. It's Only Human
13. The Natural World
14. Science and Nature
15. Famous People
16. Mixed Bag
17. Games
18. World Travel
19. Stairway to Heaven - Who Died When
20. World History
21. Fashion
22. Food and Drink
23. Pop Music
24. Sporting Terms
25. Stage and Movie Musicals
26. Books and Bookmen
27. All About Art
28. Silver Screen
29. Small Screen
30. All About Your Body
31. Wildlife
32. Science You Probably Didn't Learn at School
33. Celebs Ancient and Modern

. . . .

34.	Bits and Pieces
35.	Pot Luck
36.	Indoor Games
37.	Around the World
38.	Back In Time
39.	Getting Trendy
40.	Rock 'n' Pop
41.	Sports and Sports People
42.	Musical Theatre
43.	Olympic Firsts
44.	Novel Beginnings
45.	Sitting in the Back Row
46.	Couch Potatoes
47.	One World
48.	Flora and Fauna
49.	Simply Science
50.	People in the Past
51.	Video Games
52.	Passport Time
53.	Going Back
54.	In Its Fashion
55.	Eat Drink and Be Merry
56.	Juke Box
57.	Sports Rules, Gear & Prizes
58.	The Great White Way
59.	Gold, Silver, Bronze
60.	Popular Fiction
61.	Old and New Movies
62.	On the Box
63.	Land and Sea Creatures
64.	Sci-Fact
65.	Nothing Stranger Than Folk
66.	Route 66

67.	Pop Lyrics
68.	Gossip Column
69.	Worldwide
70.	Times Past
71.	Calorie Counting
72.	Random Rock
73.	No Business Like Showbusiness
74.	A Sporting Chance
75.	Page by Page
76.	Scenes in Cinemas
77.	Germany
78.	Italy
79.	Spain
80.	France
81.	China
82.	Canada
83.	Russia
84.	The Simpsons
85.	Rock Locations
86.	Movie Magic
87.	Channel Hopping
88.	Fur, Fin and Feather
89.	Scientific Stuff
90.	The Jacksons
91.	2015
92.	Geographical
93.	Been and Gone
94.	Liquid Refreshment
95.	Things We Wear
96.	Exotic Menu
97.	American Rock Stars
98.	More Musicals
99.	Balls

. . . .

100.	The Summer Games
101.	Writers
102.	In the Plot
103.	Painters and Paintings
104.	The Moving Image
105.	Peak Time TV
106.	Call the Doctor
107.	Animals
108.	Technology
109.	Folk Who Found Fame
110.	It's a Mad World
111.	1980s
112.	More 1980s
113.	1990s
114.	More 1990s
115.	Board Games
116.	Great for Gourmets
117.	More Tasty Treats
118.	That's Entertainment
119.	Jet Setting
120.	Yesterdays
121.	Female Fashions
122.	Hey Rock and Roll
123.	Composers
124.	You Have to be Fit
125.	Five Rings
126.	Fictional Characters
127.	India
128.	National Dishes
129.	Beatles Lyrics
130.	Stones Singles
131.	Rock Diva Lyrics
132.	National Sports

. . . .

133.	Oscars Best Actor
134.	Oscars Best Actress
135.	Rock and Roll Hall of Fame
136.	Who Said What?
137.	Young Literature
138.	Frame It
139.	Big at the Box Office
140.	Remote Control
141.	More Body Bits
142.	Ernie the Milkman
143.	Plants and Trees
144.	Domestic Science
145.	Celebrity Scandals
146.	Miscellaneous
147.	Places
148.	Comedy Songs
149.	Passing Fads
150.	The Final Countdown
152.	Tie-Break Questions
158.	Answers

More books from the Quizmaster
Available in paperback and on Kindle from Amazon

IN PURSUIT OF TRIVIA

For 25 years Brian Highley was the question writer of the many U.K. editions of Trivial Pursuit. He devised all of the questions for BBC television's Trivial Pursuit panel game, hosted by Rory McGrath. His quiz books under the Trivial Pursuit brand-name have been best-sellers across the U.K. and Europe. His more recent specialist Trivial Pursuit collector's editions based on The Rolling Stones and Classic Rock saw massive success in the USA. The on-line games Triviality and Let's Quizz! were compiled by Brian for the U.K. and North America. Brian was instrumental in launching the career of Elton John and wrote scripts for the controversial puppet satire show, Spitting Image.

COMING SOON...
The Quimaster's
Multi-choice quizbook

Printed in Poland
by Amazon Fulfillment
Poland Sp. z o.o., Wrocław

52591684R00120